# PRAISE FOR
# CALLED TO ADOPTION

*Called to Adoption, being strongly biblical, emphasizes how God's wisdom is wrapped around the heart and soul of the adoption process. I love the Adoption Wisdom sections and admonitions throughout the book; these verses capture the essence of God's love for the birth families and adoptive families. It's a wonderful book, full of biblical integrity, like a handbook and spiritual teaching guide for families hoping to adopt.*

~ Judie Sobrero, MFT

*Called to Adoption is a must read for everyone considering adoption. It's a clear, concise, easy to read step-by-step guide for everything from deciding to adopt, different ways to go about it, and how to handle situations after the adoption. Interspersed throughout the book are frequently asked questions and biblical references that will help Christians take comfort in the fact that God is in control of your adoption.*

~ Elizabeth Lowe, adoptive parent

*Thank you for an inspiring and helpful book. I particularly appreciated the scripture references and spiritual insights, as they encourage me to look back and thank God for His leading in our adoption process. Called to Adoption will help anyone get started on the road to adoption.* ~ Steve Oas, adoptive dad of two

*This book is perfect for Christian families that experience that call from God to adopt. I'm thankful that we listened to God and adopted our son! In this next adoption, everything is different. This journey has been and will be filled with lots of unknowns, but the title alone gave me encouragement that I needed and the reminder that God called me to adopt.* ~ Brandi Pierce, adoptive mother

*Knowing the quality service and tender wisdom that both Mardie and Heather bring to their work, I believe strongly that this book will arm families with the information they need to be successful in adoption. Their dedication and passion for adoption is evident in everything they do, and that clearly translates in this book.*

~ Francine D. Ward, Business & Intellectual Property Attorney

*It's wonderful. I agree with everything in this book, it's so true, so right. I hope that people will read this and understand the journey through adoption. There is a baby out there for parents who are waiting. It's in His timing. It always turns out just right. God always knows.* ~ Lonni Mayfield, adoptive mother of twins

*After reading Called to Adoption, we can really appreciate the concrete instruction about adoption and the steps that hopeful adoptive parents need to take. I think the major lesson that we learned in our adoption was to do the work that was put in front of us and to leave our hands off everything else and let God do His part. We felt a real sense of peace throughout our adoption process, mainly, I believe, because we allowed God to facilitate our adoption.* ~ Patrick and Tammy Terry, adoptive parents

*While reading this book, I was reminded of how God had a perfect plan for our lives, and there is no doubt He had a strong hand in both of our adoptions. We knew that He was leading us to adopt, and we had to trust Him through many situations that were out of our control. As with anything in life, adoption is a journey that we have to depend on God to lead the way.* ~ Lori McKenzie, adoptive mother of two and educator

*Called to Adoption is a must read for any Christian considering adoption to build their family. Mardie Caldwell and Heather Featherston have done an excellent job of outlining the major topics in adoption that must be prayerfully considered before beginning on a successful adoption journey. I only wish this book had been available to read at the beginning of our adoption journey!* ~ Tricia Davids, adoptive mother

*There are many things to think about and research prior to pursuing an adoption. Mardie lays out a plan that is Christ-centered and easy to follow. Called to Adoption is essential to helping you understand the call to adopt, the pitfalls to avoid when embarking on this journey and the steps to pursuing and completing a successful adoption like ours.* ~ Jennifer Spitzer, adoptive mother of two and educator

*What a refreshing title in today's world! This book hits on every aspect of adoption and addresses the heart issues parents face along the way. Mardie's faith and trust in God is very clear and evident in her life work in bringing children and families together. Called to Adoption is a blessing for families hoping to adopt, and I pray it will bring more couples confidently to the decision to adopt.* ~ Sarah Pulliam, adoptive mother of two

# ALSO BY MARDIE CALDWELL

*AdoptingOnline.com*

*Adoption: Your Step-by-Step Guide*

*The Healthcare Professional's Adoption Guide*

*So I Was Thinking About Adoption...*

# CALLED TO ADOPTION

A CHRISTIAN'S GUIDE TO ANSWERING THE CALL

MARDIE CALDWELL, C.O.A.P

WITH

HEATHER FEATHERSTON

American Carriage House Publishing
*Publishers Weekly* Rising Star Award Winner

Called to Adoption:
A Christian's Guide to Answering the Call
©2011 by American Carriage House Publishing

**American Carriage House Publishing**
P.O. Box 1130 Nevada City, CA 95959 U.S.A.

Library of Congress Control Number: 2010942105
Caldwell, Mardie with Featherston, Heather.
ISBN 978-1-935176-09-1 (soft cover)

Printed and bound in the United States of America

# DEDICATION

For those who have felt God's quiet urging to step out in faith and consider adopting a child into their home, their family, and their hearts for a lifetime.

*"May the Lord bless you from Zion all the days of your life;*
*may you see the prosperity of Jerusalem,*
*and may you live to see your children's children."*
Psalm 128:5-6

# TABLE OF CONTENTS

# FOREWORD

## Terry Meeuwsen

I am a HUGE adoption proponent. Five of my seven children were adopted. Every child deserves to be wanted and to have a place to belong. Spiritually, adoption is a parallel picture of how we have been adopted into the family of God.

The process of adoption is not for the faint-hearted. I actually think that's a good thing. It helps us evaluate the commitment and consider the cost. Mardie's book offers personal experiences, real stories, and valuable sources of information.

As you do your homework, listen carefully for the voice of the Lord. Adoption is a God-idea, but it is not for everyone. Be sure you and your partner are like-minded about this. You are embarking on a God-adventure. If He calls you to it, He'll provide everything you need for it. Mardie's book is a part of that provision. It's a wonderful resource. Thank you, Mardie.

*Terry Meeuwsen*
Miss America 1973
Co-host, *The 700 Club*

# ACKNOWLEDGEMENTS

We express our endless thanks for the contribution of time and talents to so many who have felt *Called to Adoption* in many different ways. The entire staff at Lifetime Adoption Center keeps the passion and ministry going each day, enabling us the time and space to speak and write. Each of them is a blessing to birth mothers and adoptive families as they help guide these precious children to the homes He has meant for them. Diane Schafer, Veronica Hofheinz, Libby Murray, Joan Oas, Lori Zandona, Jake DuCharme, Kim King, Lolita Westergren, Heidi Keefer, Jen Donnelly, Amie Weaver, D'Arce Hess, Caroline McCall, Jill Maxwell, Winona James, Diana Vandra, and Becky Tokos, this book is a tribute to your work through God's leading.

Special thanks also to Patti McKenna, our editor and designer, to Terry Meeuwsen for sharing your beautiful words, and to Lori Alarid for taking good care of us while we were so focused on this project. Thanks also to the many adoptive families who read this book and helped contribute to its creation.

The very heart of adoption is the children, and our children, Cory and Julia, Matthew and Zachary, are precious inspirations of the important role we have in God's perfect plan. Their love and support, along with that of our entire families, has encouraged us in this project and served as a constant reminder of the loving, Christian family that all children deserve.

# INTRODUCTION

"Mardie, your chances of success are one in a million," my adoption attorney warned me. However, my goal was always to become a Mommy.

I thought of everything we had already invested, questioned how much more we could go through, and still, I couldn't deny that God had a plan. Believe me, I didn't want to hire seven attorneys, but I didn't want to lose my son, either. Money was scarce at the time, and we had to make some hard decisions. We sold jewelry, personal items, and our home just to pay the adoption expenses.

My journey to motherhood included a very trying adoption experience which lasted over two years. In addition to the seven attorneys, I was working with two different states, located on opposite sides of the country. My son's birth parents changed their minds—not once, but twice!

I had no idea how this adoption was going to turn out, but I believed that the Lord wanted us to adopt this child. I knew that He would provide a way, and He did! I trusted the Lord. When I was scared or fearful, I prayed, and He comforted me and guided me with scripture. It was a difficult journey, emotionally, physically, financially, and psychologically.

It took us 18 months to finalize our adoption, but today I can confirm that it was worth everything we went through! I believe my adoption was successful because of many factors, including open communication, kindness, calmness, and faith, all provided by my Heavenly Father. I never allowed anger or resentment to enter into my adoption process. I believed, acted in faith, trusted in Him, and was blessed, just as He promised through my journey to parenthood.

Looking back, I can see that my adoption was preparing me for the work I do today, the work I began in 1986 in my living room. The Lord was truly at work in my life, and I am blessed beyond measure to have been called to a role doing His work through the miracle of Christian Adoption.

CHAPTER ONE

# ARE YOU CALLED TO ADOPTION?

*"Commit to the Lord whatever you do, and your plans will succeed."*
Proverbs 16:3

As a young, faithful wife, I looked forward to the day I would become a mother. I believed that raising children in the Lord was one of God's plans for my life. It never occurred to me that adoption would be part of His plans. As I struggled with challenges to building my family, the Lord was always faithful, opening windows when doors would close, guiding my steps through the maze that was my journey to motherhood.

Most families are built biologically, almost uneventfully through the beauty of pregnancy and God's amazing creation. Other families, however, are called to a different love through adoption. While many of us desire to be parents, I believe it is a far fewer number who are called by God to love and nurture a child who is not biologically ours. It is God who calls these parents to adoption.

Like many families, my call to adoption came after a long and disappointing journey through unsuccessful fertility treatments. I lost seven pregnancies, including miscarrying twins one Mother's Day. I never imagined this road was leading me to answer God's call in my life.

Since 1986, I have worked with thousands of couples from all backgrounds, expressing a single desire: to become parents through adoption. They all share a deep desire and belief that there is a child for them. Some had fertility issues, others did not, but they all knew with certainty that they were being led to adopt a child. I believe that this is a calling from God.

*"And whoever welcomes a little child like this*
*in my name welcomes me."*
Matthew 18:5

Are you feeling a call from the Lord to adopt? Perhaps you have a specific vision of the child that is waiting for you. Maybe you've heard stories of orphans or children in foster care who need the Godly parents you are or will become. Or maybe, like me, adoption is your hope for holding a baby in your arms—a baby that is truly yours.

## The Need for Christian Adoption

In the United States, the media and popular entertainment shows have glorified teen pregnancy. Our government is pouring out millions of dollars to support single and young mothers. However, staggering statistics have recently been released about teen parents.

- 80% of teen moms are on welfare.
- Over 50% of children raised by teen moms are reported to Child Protective Services.
- Only 1.5% of teen mothers graduate from college by age 30. And only 40% graduate from high school!
- Children raised without a father are twice as likely to quit school and four times as likely to need behavioral help.
- Children of teen parents are three times more likely to become teen parents themselves.

Internationally, the news about orphans is even worse.

- 5,760 children become orphans every day.
- Every 15 seconds, a child in Africa becomes an orphan due to AIDS.
- Worldwide, there are over 143 million children in orphanages right now.
- 10 to 15% of children raised in Eastern European orphanages commit suicide before the age of 18.
- Every 2.2 seconds, an orphan ages out of the system with no family and no home.
- In Russia, of those who age out, 60% of girls become prostitutes, 70% of boys will become hardened criminals.

As Christians, we believe the design God intended for families is optimal for children. Clearly, the statistics reflect that raising children in institutions yields disastrous results. These children are not receiving love and security, nor are they being taught self-discipline and control. More disheartening is that they likely have never heard the beautiful message of salvation through Jesus Christ.

Adoption is not only about building a family, but is also building the family of Christ. Just as we are adopted into God's family, so, too, are we called as Christians to help these children and expand Christ's territory.

## Is It Time to Answer the Call?

Many feel led to adoption or a call to help others through adoption. If you question, "Why us? Why now?," maybe the better question is, "Why not?"

Remember Jonah? He was called by God and ignored His commands because they weren't immediately comfortable. Maybe adoption seems too expensive or too difficult. Perhaps the timing doesn't seem right. Maybe you are putting it off until after the holidays, next year, or after the next milestone birthday.

Take time in God's presence to discern His will for you. If you are feeling God calling you to adopt, explore your options. Learn about the types of adoption and the choices you have. Your time spent may be to fulfill an adoption plan yourself, or it may simply be so that you are armed with accurate knowledge about Christian adoption so that you are equipped to help others.

As we go through each day, sharing His love with others, there are few ways to touch people for a lifetime. Adopting a child into our lives, our hearts, and His heavenly kingdom is actively changing a life for our lifetime and for eternity.

His plans may not be for you to adopt, but rather your actions may still fulfill His plans for a child. He may need you as an instrument to affect the lives of others.

## Steps to Successful Christian Adoptions

1. Determine the type of adoption that is best for you, including the age range and racial background of the child you want to parent.
2. Find the qualified adoption professional who will help you build your family.
3. Complete the required paperwork, profile, and other requirements to become qualified to adopt.
4. Prayerfully wait for the child God has for you, using this time of waiting to prepare for parenting.
5. Joyfully say "Yes!" when you are blessed with the opportunity to adopt a child.

## Answering Your Questions

*I feel God is calling me to become a mother again through adoption. I would especially like to adopt a child who doesn't have parents, such as through the foster system or even international adoption. My husband doesn't agree, though. He says God is calling us to be the best parents we can be to the three children we have been blessed with. Do you have any advice when a couple is conflicted about God's will for their lives?*

17

Jesus told us in Mark 3:25 that, "If a house is divided against itself, that house cannot stand." After God, your marriage and family must be the top priority in your life. Adoption should be a decision that the entire family embraces.

Continue to pray about this, and pray for God's will to be made evident to both you and your husband. In fact, I would encourage you to pray together about adoption and children in need. You may find God softens your husband's heart, or you may find He changes your vision. Either way, you need to be united in your steps to adoption for the child's sake.

As you take time in prayer, talk with your husband openly and honestly about your family. You may find his hesitation is something not related to adoption at all. Perhaps he is worried about the additional cost of raising another child, or maybe he just wishes he had more alone time with you!

*I don't know if we are called to adoption or not, but pregnancy is not happening. We are praying for guidance about in vitro fertilization (IVF), which is the next step in fertility treatments. How did you come to discover you were being called to adopt?*

I began to read, pray, and study His will for my life. Doors for a biological pregnancy were being closed, one after another. I was ready to be a mother. (See Chapter 9, A Special Note About Infertility, for my story.)

Just by reading this book, you are learning about your options, and laying them before the Lord will help you discern His will for your family.

I believe that God provides the answers if we take the time to hear Him. Offer your future family to Him in prayer, and then take time to be still and listen. Learn about IVF and your adoption options, and do not rush into either option. God will lead your footsteps.

# ADOPTION WISDOM

*"Seek justice, encourage the oppressed. Defend the cause of the fatherless, plead the case of the widow."*
**Isaiah 1:17**

We may not all be called to adopt into our own families; however, there are many things we can do to help and support families who are. As you learn more about adoption, remember those involved in adoption and consider how you can help, whether it is through volunteerism, donations, or being a prayer warrior for adoption.

CHAPTER TWO

# YOUR ADOPTION CHOICES

*"Then they would put their trust in God*
*and would not forget His deeds but would keep His commands."*
Psalms 78:7

The single most important decision you must make before beginning this path is determining the type of adoption that will be right for your family. It is a fact that the more you know, the better prepared you'll be when you need to make decisions. You should know the terminology used in different adoptions and how to avoid common pitfalls.

Through research and education, you'll be able to determine where to start, what you can afford, and a reasonable time frame for the adoption process. The Internet is an ideal place to start gathering information and reading stories about domestic and international adoption.

Today, we have access to so much help and information through the Internet. The Internet has had such a profound effect on our lives and how we do things, and adoption is no exception. Apply this technology to your adoption to save time. Get current information and reach out to the adoption professionals that are the best fit for your family, even when miles separate you. You can use online resources as you evaluate the type of adoption you desire and the adoption professionals who may be able to best help you.

As you consider your choices, I encourage you to listen to what your heart tells you. This will be a good starting point. Much of your decision may be determined by your budget, marital status, age, and desired time frame, but your heart's desire will lead you through this first step of determining the best type of adoption to pursue. The race, age, and gender of the child you hope to adopt will also play a role in determining the best path for you.

It is best to look at a variety of adoption options before starting out, speaking to other adoptive families who have recently gone though the type of adoption you are considering.

## Questions to Consider

Whether you are eager to adopt or still thinking about adoption, you may have questions that can sometimes make the process seem overwhelming.

- Do you wish to adopt a child from the United States or from another country like China, Russia, or Africa?
- Do you prefer to adopt an older child, a toddler, or a newborn?
- Do you hope to find a child who looks like you? Or a baby of another race?
- Will you use an agency, attorney, or licensed adoption facilitator?
- Do you want to do much of the leg work yourself or let the professionals do most of it?

Prayerfully consider the paths that lay before you, as well as the type of child you are open to, and proceed with faith, knowing that God will guide your adoption plan.

### Five Helpful Tips for International Adoptions

1. Use books, travel magazines, and videos to learn about the countries from which you hope to adopt your child.

2. Work with qualified professionals who have experience in adopting children from those countries.

3. Get involved with online inter-country adoption support and parenting forums.

4. Learn about the country's adoption system through recent experience of others and through your online research.

5. Find local, positive support groups for people who have adopted from your child's country by searching online and through local churches.

## International Adoption

International adoption is defined as an adoption where the child lives outside of the United States and is a citizen of another country.

Sometimes international adoption provides more options for prospective parents, such as adoption of an older child or gender specification. Some countries may have more restrictions and eligibility requirements than domestic organizations, but others may be more open. Also, because of the complexity of international adoption, the risk of a birth parent coming to reclaim the child is slim.

Over the course of the last decade, the number of children involved in international adoptions has increased dramatically. Asian-born children from countries such as China, Vietnam, and South Korea top the list of the most common international adoptions. Ethiopia, Russia, Kazakhstan, and Ukraine follow.

Before you move forward with an international adoption, it is important to gather information and support. One way to do this is to become involved with an international adoption support group or parent group. You can do this online, or if there are groups in your area, attend meetings in your city.

## WHEN DISASTER STRIKES

Often after a disaster in another country, such as an earthquake or hurricane, hundreds of people will contact the government's social defense department inquiring about adopting. At our center, we are flooded with calls after disasters when the pictures and stories of abandoned children are making news. There is a wonderful outpouring of love toward children shown in these images; however the problem is that the process is not an easy one. Children have to be considered orphans before they can be adopted, and then the paperwork is handled just like any other adoption.

Many big-hearted people don't understand you just can't fly over to a country and bring back a planeload of needy children. There are costs involved with the orphanage, travel, and legal and medical expenses, as well as an abundance of paperwork needed to make the adoption legal. Some of these children are cared for by relatives or other families right after a disaster strikes. Other children are on their own until they are found.

For people reacting to a disaster, we welcome them to consider adoption, but remind them to remember that an emotional decision is not always the best motivator for this lifelong commitment. Immediate assistance can be provided through donations of money or goods to one of the many international aid organizations, such as the Red Cross.

There are decisions to make before proceeding, such as the country you wish to adopt from, your budget, the time you can afford to spend overseas, and more. All will affect your options. Bear in mind that changing plans midway through international adoption may require back-tracking or possibly starting over.

International adoption is not without risk. Countries are constantly opening and closing their doors to adoption. For example, Haiti, an attractive option for Christian parents, saw its international adoption program halted by a devastating earthquake in 2010.

Countries can also add additional restrictions at any time, such as China did, rendering some parents-in-waiting no longer eligible to adopt. Still others, like Guatemala, can shut down completely due to fraud. Families in the adoption process can find their plans abruptly stopped due to political elements beyond their control.

To best prepare, take time now to read and study. Learn about international adoption restrictions, including those relative to travel, and find a way to stay updated. An additional risk is simply the unknown. Adoptive parents have traveled to meet their child, only to find out that the child had many more medical or special needs than they were led to believe. Some found peace in their faith and moved forward. Others felt deceived and unprepared to bring home ill children, such as HIV positive babies or those afflicted with cerebral palsy.

Research your options, read the fine print, and talk to other adoptive parents who have had both good experiences and difficult adoptions internationally. You must be very clear with your spouse and yourself about what you can handle. Adoption should not be a purely emotional decision. Remember, this is a lifetime commitment.

## Medical Concerns

In the many years I have worked with adoptive families, I have found that many wear rose-colored glasses when they view a photograph of their prospective child from overseas. The big pleading eyes of an orphan can pull at sympathetic hearts, and sometimes it's only after they bring the child home that they see that poor diet, neglect, and unsanitary living conditions have caused chronic disorders. I can't tell you how many times I've heard, "But they told me she'd be just fine with some good food and love."

The children came to the orphanage because they were abandoned; their parents died or were sick or too poor to provide for them. They likely receive little medical care, may be malnourished or have parasites, or even tuberculosis, developmental delays, or behavioral problems. When your agency finds a child for you to consider, they should send you a referral that includes a child's medical file, background information, and photographs. Choose an agency that will send you a current videotape of the child and any medical reports needing to be translated. Seek out a physician experienced with inter-country adoption.

Paul and Sara were a Christian couple who, in their college years, had both spent time serving in church missions overseas. They had agreed, even before they were married, that they would build their family through international adoption. They completed an adoption of two Ukrainian little boys. When I met Paul and Sara, they were beginning a support group for local families who had adopted from Eastern Europe and Russia.

"We were so naïve," Sara shared with me. "We thought that love and a Christian home environment would be the foundation to helping Alex and Peter blossom. Thankfully, both boys are now doing well, but for the first twelve months, Paul and I truly didn't know if we could become a family."

The boys, both deemed healthy by the orphanage, each had varied needs and diagnoses that included fetal alcohol syndrome, delayed development, attachment issues, and malnutrition. After a difficult first year, the family was beginning to find a balance, a routine, and a normal family life.

"I suppose they were seen as normal children in the orphanage, but unfortunately that left us ill-prepared to be parents to our children," Sara said. "I believe all families looking into international adoption should expect certain issues and learn about them. If your child has them, you are blessed because you are prepared. If not, then you are doubly blessed!"

## Domestic Adoption

Domestic adoption is an adoption that takes place between citizens of the United States. There can be travel involved, although it is within the U.S. There are decisions to make about the type of domestic adoption you desire, including the relationship you are comfortable having with your child's birth family, the type of adoption professional you want to help you, and how to present yourself to potential birth parents.

Within the U.S., adoption laws vary from state to state and are constantly changing. This provides adopting parents a variety of options. For instance, an adoptive family may be from Texas and the birth mother who chose them could be in California. Attorneys will look at the laws in both states to determine the various options and which laws will take precedence in the adoption.

The laws recognize two basic types of domestic adoption, which differ by how birth parents consent to the adoption. With an agency adoption, birth parents relinquish parental rights to an agency that then places the child with an approved family for adoption. Through private or independent adoptions, birth parents give parental rights directly to the adoptive parents they have chosen.

In any agency adoption, the parental rights are either voluntarily surrendered or have been terminated by the court, in cases of neglect or abuse, for example.

Public agencies are usually operated by social service departments and place children with special needs. Private agencies, licensed or supervised by the states, are for-profit or non-profit and tend to specialize in foreign born, special

### The Seven Steps to International Adoption

1. Choose an experienced, qualified adoption professional.

2. Complete all of the required paperwork and become eligible to adopt.

3. Be referred for a child and accept the referral.

4. Apply for the child to be eligible to immigrate to the U.S.

5. Adopt the child legally.

6. Obtain an immigrant visa, birth certificate, and U.S. passport for the child.

7. Once these steps are completed, the child may legally enter the United States.

8. Re-adopt the child here in the U.S., using the laws of your state. (This step, while legally optional, is highly recommended in order for your child to have all the rights and privileges of a family member.)

needs, or minority children and, sometimes, in infants. Agencies typically operate only on a local level. (See Chapter 3, Getting Started, for more information.)

## Agency vs. Private Adoption

In an **AGENCY ADOPTION,** the child is legally and often physically relinquished to an adoption agency. The agency then places the child with a qualified adoptive family of the agency's choosing. (There are times, through an IDENTIFIED AGENCY ADOPTION, that the birth mother may choose the family.)

In **PRIVATE OR INDEPENDENT ADOPTION,** the birth parents legally transfer their parental rights directly to the adoptive parents that they have chosen and may choose to place the baby directly into their arms. This type of adoption allows many more choices for both birth families and adoptive couples.

When the birth parents relinquish rights directly to adoptive parents through independent adoption, the laws call it direct placement. Some state laws are virtually silent on this practice, while others regulate it closely. Most states provide that an intermediary, such as a lawyer or licensed adoption facilitator, can help arrange independent adoptions. Independent adoptions can be completed more quickly and usually are less expensive than agency adoptions.

This is important: You need to choose an adoption professional who specializes in the type of adoption you want, who has a good track record, and with whom you feel comfortable with on the intimate level required for adoption. This is true when selecting adoption attorneys, as well.

Because of the nature of domestic adoption, a local office is not required for any service other than the home study, which needs to be in your state. In today's adoptions, many families choose the professional best suited to their needs, which may be out of state. For example, our center is in California, yet families come to us from across the country, and even around the world if they are military families stationed overseas.

In difficult economic times, often public assistance is reduced and women look instead to make direct placement adoption plans, rather than risk foster care involvement. With private adoption, they can make a conscious, thoughtful adoption plan, choosing the type of family they desire and placing their child directly in the arms of that family.

As you research adoption professionals, ask them about their birth mother outreach. If it is a nationwide organization, ask if you will be presented to birth mothers across the country. Some large agencies have many offices but only represent adoptive families to their own local birth mothers, which can limit your opportunities and extend your wait time.

Alisha called our center late one night, after everyone at her home was asleep. She was a 19-year-old college student from Dallas, and about eight months pregnant. She had hid her pregnancy from her family and now desperately was hoping to make an adoption plan.

"I want a Christian couple who can come to the hospital," she told me in hushed tones. "I just can't bring the baby home. Can you help me find someone who can do that? Who can be close by when I'm due? And who don't live anywhere around here? I just can't risk my parents finding out. They would be so disappointed in me."

I assured her that we could definitely help her with that. After viewing waiting families on our website, Alisha chose a family from the northeast who were thrilled to be able to help and support her during her last weeks of pregnancy. She delivered right on time with the adoptive mother in the delivery room, acting as her labor support person.

Alisha's plan went just as she wanted, a testimony to the choices available through private adoption.

## Open, Semi-Open, and Closed Adoptions

With an **OPEN ADOPTION**, birth parents have the opportunity to select the family who will parent their child. The adoptive parents and birth parents may speak, meet, and get to know each other before the birth, and then communicate afterwards, as well. As the birth mother progresses in her pregnancy, she can send ultrasound photos and share additional photos, if desired.

There is a trust on both sides of adoption, and typically all parties feel as though this is a special journey, creating a relationship that is best for the child in the long term.

| TYPES OF ADOPTION | |
|---|---|
| **OPEN** | Birth parents may select adopting family.<br>Free exchange of information and identification.<br>Communication during pregnancy and after birth is common. |
| **SEMI-OPEN** | Birth parents may select adopting family.<br>Some exchange of information, sometimes through a third party.<br>Communication during pregnancy and after birth, if desired. |
| **CLOSED** | No identifying information is shared.<br>No contact between birth parents and adoptive parents during pregnancy or after birth.<br>Records are often sealed. |

Communication after adoption can take many forms. These can include communication via a website, (such as a social networking site or a private web site), text messaging, email, phone calls, and even old fashioned letters and pictures sent in the mail. Visits after adoption may occur, but are usually casual in nature and do not involve leaving the child alone with the birth family. They involve the birth mother (or birth family) getting together with the adoptive parents and the child for lunch, a visit at a park, or perhaps even a day at a county fair, for example. Open adoption is not co-parenting, but can be seen as more people to love your child.

**Easy Ideas for Ongoing Communication in an Open or Semi-Open Adoption**

1. Mail letters and photos to the birth mother, either directly or send them through your adoption professional.

2. Email, instant message, or text message with the birth mother.

3. Create a website, blog, or social networking account online for the birthmother to view your updates. Make the site private if you want to limit access.

4. Connect occasionally through phone calls or video calls via the Internet.

5. Coordinate annual visits.

**SEMI-OPEN ADOPTION** involves the sharing of some information, but not necessarily identifying information. For example, a birth mother may choose the adoptive family but may not know their last names, state of residence, or have their direct phone number. Open communication may exist, but it can be through email or a third party, such as your adoption professional. It can even be in the form of adoptive parents communicating with the birth grandparents of the child, rather than the birth mother.

As you think about it, you may feel some fear or discomfort about committing to ongoing communication with someone you don't know, but experience can soften our hearts and bring us to the understanding that birth families typically want contact because they, too, love this child.

**Helpful Tip:**
When you take photos, have a couple extra printed and drop them into a waiting card and envelope for your birth mother. Then, you'll be prepared when it is time to send an update. When you send that card, start a new card immediately so it is ready to receive your new photos. This makes it easy to keep your commitment.

In most circumstances, semi-open adoption can change to become more open as the relationship develops between adoptive parents and a child's birth family, if mutually agreed upon.

Ron and Liz were open to a semi-open adoption, sending photos and letters through our adoption center. They clearly stated that they were not comfortable with more, nor were they open to occasional visits. They were chosen by Renee, a teenage birth mother who preferred no ongoing communication whatsoever.

At the hospital, as Ron and Liz were awaiting their son's birth, they met Renee's parents and instantly hit it off! Both couples were in their early 40's, and during the long labor, learned that they had a lot in common. A few days later, when it was time for the baby to be discharged, Ron and Liz realized that they wanted to see Renee's family. Now, more than six years later, they still spend a week each summer together.

"We weren't looking for a relationship like that," Ron shares. "But God had it waiting for us! They are part of our son's family, and He opened our hearts to see that they are now part of our family, too. We didn't know what He had in store. Adoption has been a life-changing experience for us."

In the case of a domestic adoption where there is little contact with the birth mother, you can still gather enough information to be able to answer questions your child will have. In adopting a foreign-born child, you will learn very little about the birth parents, but you can usually discover enough about the village the child came from or the circumstance that brought him to the orphanage or foster care. Children who grow up knowing that they were adopted by honest, trustworthy, and supportive parents will grow up with a healthier sense of self.

As a Christian and an adoption professional, I believe that open or semi-open adoptions are most beneficial for all involved. The birth mother has the peace she needs that her child is happy and healthy, and that she made the right decision. The adoptive parents have access to the birth family should they need medical information or have other questions. And the child has the opportunity to know that his adoption was a choice made out of great love, with a birth mother who cared more about him than her own desires, and that his adoptive parents embrace not only him, but his biological heritage, as well. I have found, too, that parenting is less stressful and fears are calmed when the birth mother is known, embraced, and available.

*Rely on Him when you feel doubt or need strength. He has all we need.*

*"The Sovereign Lord is my strength; He makes my feet like the feet of a deer, He enables me to go on the heights."*
Habakkuk 3:19

Oftentimes, God is more in tune with what would be good for us and our adoption. Allow Him to prepare your heart for the adoption He knows you can handle. This can mean putting your emotions aside until you find peace, as I did in my adoption. The benefits far outweigh any risk.

A **CLOSED, CONFIDENTIAL, OR TRADITIONAL ADOPTION** is one in which there is no identifying information shared with anyone who is a party to adoption. There is typically little information available, and later on, sealed or destroyed records may make it impossible to learn much more than basic medical information or other minor details for the child.

In a closed adoption, there is no contact between the birth parents and adoptive parents either before or after the adoption, and the child may never have opportunity to find his biological family, if he desires.

Hopeful adoptive parents seeking an adoption like this are encouraged to explore why they may have fears of birth parents or want no contact, as closed adoption is not considered to be in the best interest of children. Most adoption professionals know from personal experience and from research that it's a disservice to an adopted child if his parents do not have adequate information to share about his birth parents and why he was placed for adoption. When he asks a simple question about his heritage, for the sake of his emotional health, parents cannot respond with secrecy, lies, or blank stares.

Consider Jacob, who was adopted through a closed adoption. As he approached the age of 18, his mother discussed with him the opportunities of filing with the adoption agency to get information about or to contact his birth parents, if that was his desire.

"Why would I want to do that?" he asked. "She never cared about what happened to me."

Despite explanations to the contrary, Jacob truly believed that the lack of information about his birth family was because they didn't love or want him. In his mind, if they could give him away so easily, he didn't want them to be a part of his life and found it difficult to discuss his feelings surrounding adoption.

Closed adoption does not provide the framework for an understanding of the circumstances surrounding adoption choices or the opportunity for reassurance. If, after learning the facts and praying about it, you still feel the desire for a closed adoption, explore the international adoption of orphans. Continue to prayerfully consider this choice, and do not choose closed adoption simply out of fear.

*"I will give you a new heart and put a new spirit in you;*
*I will remove from you your heart of stone*
*and give you a heart of flesh."*
Ezekiel 36:26

# Adopting a Foster Child

Each year, state child welfare workers investigate some four million cases where parents or guardians abuse, neglect, or otherwise mistreat children, or who lack the skills or resources to cope with a child's medical conditions or emotional or psychological problems. 580,000 of these children are removed from their homes and placed with foster parents or relatives, in institutions, group homes, or residential treatment centers. There they may remain for an average of two years, but it is not uncommon for a child to remain in the foster care system for five to seven years. As a former foster mother, I believe that this temporary environment is not in the best interest of children for the long term.

Difficult circumstances compel social workers to move many of the children from one temporary foster placement to another. Meanwhile, they try to help birth parents resolve problems like drug and alcohol abuse or domestic violence so they can reunify them with their children. Should reunification fail, they initiate legal action to terminate parental rights and seek permanent placement of the child outside the home.

In recent years, both the federal government and most states have made adopting foster children easier and more affordable. For example, California has:

- Simplified home study reports.
- Implemented financial assistance to many foster parents who adopt foster children.
- Complied with the financial incentives of federal statutes that require a state plan to provide foster families with financial adoption assistance.
- Made post-adoption funds available, especially to foster families adopting special-needs children.

It is important to note, however, that foster parenting is not always a path to adoption. Inquire about the Fost-Adopt program if you are interested in adopting through the foster care system.

Many families seek a local public agency to complete a low- or no-cost adoption through foster care, only to learn later that the wait is long if they want a child under the age of two. If you truly want to parent a child that is in need, adopting a waiting child in the U.S. is a wonderful way to do it.

Please keep in mind, that just because adoption through the foster system is low-cost, it should not be pursued primarily for that reason. I've spoken with hundreds of families who were willing to wait a long time for a free infant adoption through the state. After years of waiting without success, they realized the time spent waiting was time lost with a child, and suddenly the price seemed very high.

Remember, in many cases of foster care, children are reunited with their birth parents or placed in other adoptive homes. Nonetheless, if you are a foster parent who would like to adopt the child or children in your care, it is certainly in your best interest to speak with the appropriate agencies involved in your specific case. To learn more about foster care in your area, I encourage you to seek out foster parents in your church or other local churches. You will learn much from their experiences.

If you are open to an older child, there are many children lost in the foster care system who are desperate for loving homes. An older child adoption can sometimes be quicker than a newborn match, but the paperwork might be lengthier. This is because there are often more records to obtain and review, including medical, psychiatric, and school reports. Sibling matches are also quicker, because so few adoptive parents want to adopt two or more children at once. There is a need for families to adopt older children from foster care because most hopeful parents want to adopt a newborn.

## Adopting Within Your Family

At times, an adoption need arises within a family. Perhaps death, substance usage, or poor choices have created a situation that leaves a child needing more stability than mom or dad can provide. One question must weigh heavier than all others: what is in the child's best interest? While there are certainly cases in which adoption is emotionally and financially precisely what the child needs, it should always be carefully considered well in advance of the start of the process.

Depending on the reasons why, placing a child for adoption outside of the family may be a consideration, especially if a birth parent has emotionally or physically harmed a child. In my experience, adoption within the family is not usually the best choice. While it may feel more drastic to look outside the family, this is often a more emotionally stable option for the child. Adoption by a new family, away from the negative behavior or influence, can be the greatest gift a child can receive.

For instance, many years ago, I was contacted by Maria, who was looking for an adoptive family for her son, Miguel. He had been sexually abused, and she was desperate to get him to a better family. Maria's parents had offered to adopt him, but she felt strongly, as did I, that he would be better in a new family with no ties to the abuser. He needed a family who could embrace him and help him build a life without fear and constant reminders of the abuse he'd endured. The only way to do this was by placing him with someone who was not a member of his family.

If you are faced with a similar decision about a possible adoption within your own family, ask yourself a few questions:

- Is continued contact with the birth family something that is in this child's best interests?
- Will the child get mixed messages about their adoption?
- Is the birth mother or birth father someone who should be involved in this child's life?
- Will the boundaries be clear between birth parents and adopting parents?
- Is it in the best interest of this child to be raised within the family?
- Would a private adoption with an approved and ready adoptive family be a better fit for the child at this time?

Even though adoption is permanent, it can be confusing when a birth parent is still around or remains in the picture in some way. For example, a couple who was waiting with our center to adopt was asked by a niece to adopt the baby boy she was carrying. They prayerfully considered it, but eventually declined, referring her instead to other waiting families with Lifetime.

When we discussed the situation together, they shared that it all just felt too close for comfort. While they knew they could love and successfully parent her baby, they also thought that this child deserved a home without constant fear of the birth mother intervening simply because she has complete access. Also, their niece had other children from previous relationships and expressed a desire to "keep the kids together," another warning flag for these adoptive parents.

In the end, she chose another couple and has a wonderful open relationship, which includes annual visits. The roles are very clear, and her son is now growing up happy and safe, without confusion or drama that are often characteristic of adoption within the family.

## Special Needs Adoption

Special needs children usually have varying degrees of physical, mental, or emotional challenges. They include school-age children who were neglected and have learning disabilities, or adolescents who were traumatized by sexual abuse and have psychological disorders. Others may have physical conditions like Down's Syndrome or cerebral palsy. Some, born addicted to drugs, are at risk of eventual physical and emotional difficulties.

Many children with special needs will struggle with the effects of mistreatment or physical challenges through childhood and often throughout their lives. They require adoptive parents who can provide them with stability and structure, special care and professional help, patience and love, and the Lord's guidance.

# Helpful Tips for Adopting a Child with Special Needs...

- Do not jump in just because you hear of a child in need. Take time to pray and decide if this is the adoption to which you've been called.

- Observe and talk with parents who are raising a child who has needs similar to the child you might adopt.

- Think about the severity of the disabilities and behavioral problems you can handle—don't take on more because you feel sorry for a child.

- Be prepared. Enroll in instructional parenting classes available locally or online. Read books recommended by your adoption home study provider.

- Visit Internet forums to read about adoptive parents whose lives are filled with purpose and joy after special needs adoptions. Also, learn from those who are struggling.

- Seek guidance by emailing and relating to parents you meet online who've *been there and done that.*

- Make sure you apply for the Adoption Assistance Program (AAP), a government financial assistance program for adopting a child with special needs.

- Always finalize a special needs adoption through an agency, even if an attorney or facilitator has located a child for you. This is required to qualify for AAP in most adoptions.

- Search the Internet for information about your child's condition, new treatment methods, and expert advice. Also search for medical resources, equipment, and supplies.

- Commit yourself to providing the quality of life, patience, understanding, unconditional love, and spiritual guidance your child deserves.

- If your agency requires counseling for your family to adopt a special needs child, accept it graciously and don't be offended, because it will help you all.

- Stay in touch with social workers and adoption professionals for guidance and to help you adjust to your new reality.

- Learn new skills to meet the child's needs and be prepared to make a lifelong commitment.

- Do your praying <u>now</u> so you are in tune with the Lord's leading.

## EVERY CHILD IS ADOPTABLE

Our local hospital is quite small, and one night they called with a request for help. They had a young woman deliver twin boys, hoping to make a last minute adoption plan for them both to go to the same home. Normally, this would have been a fairly common request; however, in this case, one of the boys had spina bifida. When we received the call, he had already been flown to the regional children's hospital and was in surgery for the softball-size hole in his back. Because his birth mother had received no prenatal care, this condition was a complete surprise.

A wonderful waiting couple stepped forward in faith to adopt these boys. Dad was a pastor; Mom was a nurse prior to giving up her career to stay home with their daughter. They eagerly accepted the twins with no hesitation, knowing that this was the Lord's plan for their family. Today, both boys are doing well, exploring their rural home in Alaska. The treatment for spina bifida is ongoing, but the boy affected is walking and doing most all the things that a little five-year-old boy should be doing! The Lord has called this family together and blessed them for their readiness to accept His plan.

# Trans-Racial Adoptions

When a family adopts a child that is a different race than their own, it is considered a trans-racial adoption. Currently, we are seeing this in the adoption of African American children by Caucasian families, through both domestic and international adoptions. Not only is this a trend in Christian homes, but high-profile celebrity adoptions are also setting examples. Sandra Bullock, Angelina Jolie, and Katherine Heigl have all recently adopted children with an ethnic heritage different than their own.

While you may be completely prepared for this, you will need to ensure that your family is prepared, as well. Ted and Amanda were open to a child of any race and were chosen by an African American birth mother to adopt her baby. Brought up in Christian homes, they never imagined that their families would have anything but love for their baby. Imagine their surprise when an uncle and a cousin both made racial slurs about their baby at the family gathering designed to welcome the baby home! Have these family conversations well in advance. You don't need to change your plans based solely on your family's approval, but you should be aware of their view. It may be an opportunity to pray for God's change in their hearts.

Similarly, you should evaluate if you have resources in your city or county to expose a child to their heritage and others that share their ethnicity. It may seem odd when they are quite young, but when they begin to ask questions about why they look different than you, it will help you explain if you also have places to go and things to share to support your child as he grows up confident as the individual he is and as part of your family.

Your adoption home study provider may require or recommend classes for families open to adopting outside of their race. You should actively participate and ask questions so you will be prepared later. Seek out programs or support groups for families built through trans-racial adoption. If these are not available in your area, consider attending a church with diversity and programs available to support your child's need for identity and belonging.

Here are a few important questions to ask yourself if you are considering trans-racial adoption:

- How will you help your child be comfortable growing up in your hometown?
- Do you already know people of diversity or who may share the same race as your child? Will you need to make new connections to expand your social circle for your child and family's well-being?
- Do you know of support or play groups for trans-racial families created through adoption? If not, would you be comfortable starting one?
- Does your neighborhood or city hold cultural celebrations? Attend, introduce yourself, and get involved.
- What are ways you'll honor, respect, and celebrate your child's difference within your family? Books, dolls, play groups, and other avenues are available to help a child identify with and embrace their unique racial differences in a positive way.

## Answering Your Questions

*We are specifically hoping to adopt a girl. We've heard it is easier in international adoption. Is that true?*

Yes, especially if the country allows only one biological child per family, like China for example. The birth parents may abandon or place for adoption their female child, hoping the next birth will be a male. Many cultures feel a male child is more capable of caring for his parents than a female.

Also, because international adoptions are of children who are already born, gender specification is very common and usually allowed.

Some domestic adoption professionals do allow families to specifically request a boy or girl. You'll need to ask the agency, attorney, or adoption facilitator to find out if they have restrictions on gender preference.

*Is closed adoption without any birth parent contact easier to obtain in another country?*

If fear of openness and relating to a birth mother occupy your thoughts, you need to learn why and to resolve this issue before you adopt any child. Some adoptive parents are terribly afraid that a birth mother may try to reclaim her baby. They often think they would feel more secure adopting a child abandoned to an orphanage, mother unknown. And it is true that most international adoptions are, indeed, closed. Unfortunately for your child, you may not have much to share about his or her origins; this difficulty is slowly changing, but it is something we must accept in adopting internationally.

Domestically, few adoption professionals provide closed and sealed adoptions any longer. If this is indeed your desire, speak with other parents who have closed adoptions, and seek out the other side, as well. There are stories from grown children of adoption, birth mothers, and families that will help you decide what works best for your family.

### Are international adoptions more difficult than domestic U.S. adoptions?

You will find you find there are difficulties and blessings in both international and domestic adoptions. There are many differences regarding the paperwork, time frame, and expectations. Expenses can be more in an international adoption with travel and longer stays required.

The most important steps you can take to help avoid difficulties is to do your research in advance. Speak to other parents and adoptive families that have adopted from the specific country you are considering, learn about the customs, buy a book about the country, join an online support group for this specific country, and purchase a dictionary or audio program with terms in the native language of the country. Remember to choose an experienced adoption organization with a proven track record in your particular country of interest. Use the Better Business Bureau Online to identify professionals with a solid record.

### Is it difficult to adopt a healthy newborn in the U.S.?

No, this is actually a myth. There are thousands of adoptions each year of healthy newborns in the U.S. There are babies of all races, adopted nationwide, typically through private agencies, licensed adoption facilitators, or adoption attorneys.

### Is open adoption confusing for a child?

No, in fact, it is typically far less confusing than closed adoption. Consider this: rather than spending their whole lives wondering about their birth parents and the circumstances of their adoption, they know their story.

When adoption is explained from a very early age, it seems completely normal to a child. You are mom and dad; the fact that they grew in someone's womb is simply biology. Open adoption offers them a chance to know their "tummy mommy" and why she chose *you* as their parents.

# ADOPTION WISDOM

*Don't stop seeking His face. Continue to grow in faith and in wisdom.*

*"I love those who love me, and those who seek me will find me."*
**Proverbs 8:17**

As you consider your adoption choices, you may find your heart opening in ways you did not expect. You may feel more open in the type of child you are considering, or you may be surprised by the specific desires you have. There is no right or wrong answer in adoption preferences.

Lay all of your decisions at the feet of God. Continue to pray over them. In many cases, such as preferences for race or gender, you are able to expand your search if you feel God's leading.

CHAPTER THREE

# GETTING STARTED

*"If the Lord delights in a man's way, He makes his steps firm."*
Psalm 37:23

Most of the first steps toward adoption take place at home in deciding the type of adoption God is calling you toward. Taking time, having open conversations, spending time in prayer and in the Word will all help you determine the path to take toward your child and your future.

Once you have made your decisions, you will need to begin the process of finding the professionals you need to help you. You'll need to find those who specialize in the type of adoption you want.

For instance, if you are pursuing a domestic, newborn adoption, be sure the organization you choose works directly with their own birth mothers and has the support system in place for them. You don't want your adoption coordinator jetting off to work on an international adoption just as your baby is due. Similarly, if you are seeking an adoption internationally, find a professional who has experience working in the country you have chosen, who has good connections, and who can walk you through the entire adoption.

So how do you research adoption professionals? How do you determine who to trust with your adoption journey? How do you even know what you need? Begin by identifying potential adoption professionals by Internet research, asking other adoptive families, and learning who is out there. (See Adoption Resources in the back of this book.)

## Public and Private Agency Adoptions

Nearly two-thirds of all adoptions are arranged through some type of agency. Public agencies are licensed and run by the state, county, or city, and are funded by tax dollars. The children they represent tend to be older and may face emotional challenges or disabilities. In public agency adoptions, the identity of the birth parents may not be disclosed. Fees are usually very low or nonexistent, making public adoption a viable option for those who would otherwise be limited due to financial issues.

Private and independent agencies operate differently from public agencies and can be either for profit or nonprofit. Funding comes from the adoptive parents and, in some cases, from limited grants and donations. These agencies bring together birth parents and potential adoptive parents, and they sometimes allow the birth mother to choose who will adopt her child.

It is critical that potential adoptive parents do their homework carefully and thoroughly to be certain that they choose the type of agency best suited to their needs.

## Know the Facts

Before you hire anyone, understand what your adoption professional stands for.

Unfortunately, not all adoption agencies and professionals with Christian names are actually Christian organizations. They may have been purchased by an organization and retained the name. Ask for a mission statement or a statement of faith if you aren't sure.

Similarly, whether an organization is non-profit or for-profit should not be any determination of its values, nor does it mean that the fees are less or the service is better. State law and accounting practice often determine tax status, as well as how the company can operate in your best interest.

## What You Should Know about Adoption Agencies

- Public or state adoption agencies tend to cost less.

- Public adoption agencies often do not allow contact with the birth parents or a lot of disclosure regarding the history of the birth family.

- Public adoption agencies usually represent older children or children who may have special needs.

- Independent adoption agencies must be licensed.

- An adoption home study is conducted, regardless of the type of adoption you choose.

- Always thoroughly investigate private and independent agencies before selecting services.

## Licensed Adoption Facilitators

Since the 1980s, adoption facilitators have played an important role in bringing together birth and adoptive parents. They often accomplish the task much more quickly than private or public agencies. Regulation and licensing of adoption facilitators varies from state to state. Ask the individual organizations about their qualifications. It's best to use licensed, registered, and established adoption facilitators.

Birth mothers often prefer working through adoption facilitators because they are able to complete private adoptions, where they relinquish their parental rights directly to the adoptive family, rather than to an organization. They are able to make more decisions about their adoption, their child, and the type of ongoing contact they desire. They are able to complete a more personalized adoption, while still taking advantage of the services available through an adoption professional without any cost to them. It's simply easier to have a customized adoption plan.

In 2008, I worked diligently to help establish the licensing requirements for adoption facilitators in California. After working for so many years and helping thousands of families adopt, this opportunity was priceless. I was the only adoption professional asked to speak before the state legislature about the need for the requirements. What a thrill it was when Governor Schwarzenegger signed the bill into law later that year!

One of the biggest differences between adoption agencies and facilitators is their focus. Agencies tend to be more local and adoptive-family focused since they provide a full-service type package, including the adoption home study to the adoptive family. Adoption facilitators tend to be more birth mother focused and are able to work nationwide. This is often a key to success because the time is spent in caring for women considering adoption, rather than time spent in the field providing home studies for adoptive families.

Adoption facilitators also typically have well-developed referrals they can provide to you for home study and legal services. Because of the differences in focus, facilitators tend to complete more adoptions than agencies and typically work with far more potential birth mothers.

## Private Adoptions

Private, also known as independent, adoptions can take several forms. You may choose to work through an adoption attorney, an agency, an adoption facilitator, or any combination of professionals. While it is possible to find a birth parent on your own, the time and effort involved can be daunting. For that reason, most individuals who opt for independent adoption also choose to use an intermediary of some kind.

The advantages of using intermediaries, such as adoption facilitators or attorneys, for a private adoption include:

- Access to more potential birth parents
- A greater chance of being selected for a child sooner
- Help in handling the maze of adoption paperwork
- Less chance of details being overlooked
- More personalized services for both adoptive parents and birth parents

Remember that services included will vary from one professional to another. Always verify what is included and what is not included.

## Hiring an Adoption Professional

Interview adoption professionals as you start your search for someone to help you build your family through adoption:

- How long have you been in the adoption profession?
- How did you first become involved in adoption? Why?
- What services do you provide, both for adoptive parents and for birth parents?
- What services don't you provide?
- What are your fees? When are they due?
- What is your particular area of expertise?
- Do you have a formal contract?
- Depending on the type of service that is offered, are you licensed, bonded, or certified?
- What is your success rate, and in what time frame can the average family expect to adopt?
- Do you have an open door policy? Can we tour your facility?
- How many adoptions do you complete a year?
- What are your hours? Can you be reached after hours and on weekends or holidays?
- How do you primarily communicate with waiting adoptive families? With birth parents?

The best tools you will use while conducting your adoption research are the notes and files you will keep during your search. Keep hard copies or electronic files. Your files should include all the information, literature, and notes you have obtained on the professional you are considering. Keep a list of dates and the names of the people you speak to.

I recommend you also write down how the phone conversation went. Did they answer the phone with a live person, or did you have to leave a message during regular hours? Was their website informative, updated, and helpful? Did it have broken links or old information? What type of track record do they have in adoption success? Did you feel valued and encouraged when you hung up?

Take steps to do common sense investigation, too, such as:

- Check out the Better Business Bureau and/or licensing board.
- Ask for references and check them out.

- Review any agreement or contract with an independent adoption attorney.
- Learn about the size of the staff, how after-hours calls are handled, and other services that may affect your adoption. This is very important if you need to speak with someone urgently about your own adoption.
- Research the organization from a birth parent's perspective. How does it feel? Would you call them?

Working with an adoption professional in another state is very common and easy with the use of the Internet. With planning, patience, and the determination to follow through on your information, you should feel confident in the adoption professional you finally select. You will save time, money, and frustration when you plan and use the questions above. Your research will become invaluable to you and your adoption success.

At our center, we work around the clock with both adoptive families and prospective birth parents across the country. Through the internet, email, instant message, live chat, 24-hour phone lines, Skype, mail, and in person meetings, our staff truly meets clients where they are. Communication is one of the main keys to adoption success. This is the time to do your research, ask questions, and consider an adoption professional from all sides as you make your selection.

Remember to include God in your decision-making process. Pray over your work. Pray for the adoption professionals you come in contact with. Let the Lord guide your steps to adoption and follow His call.

## The Adoption Home Study

In most states, a social worker will evaluate your fitness to parent during what's known as a home study. Rather than a study and evaluation of your home, it's really a people study. Adoption home studies not only serve to qualify you to adopt, but also help to prepare you for adoptive parenting...for the child you're so eager to meet!

Requirements in each state differ, but an adoption home study usually includes a home inspection, physicals, a review of your finances, references from friends and coworkers, and a background report that may include an FBI check. It also includes personal interviews with everyone living in your home and a little personal history about your family life.

Nearly all people who apply to adopt do qualify for a home study, and most prospective parents worry unnecessarily. The intent of a home study is to screen out people with severe mental illness, drug or alcohol dependency, a criminal record of child abuse, or those with so little income that an adopted child would be placed into poverty. If your home life is stable, if you are in reasonably good health, if you have enough income to raise a child, and if you are a loving and responsible person with a heartfelt desire to parent a child for life, you should qualify to adopt.

Adoption home studies should be kept updated. In most states, families only need to update annually. Check with your home study provider to make sure your report is kept current so you don't compromise a potential adoption. Even ordinary changes in your life need to be reflected by a home study update, including moving to a different home, changing jobs, having a relative move into your home, adding a biological child, or if you change your preferences for a child.

After you are home with your child, your home study provider will visit you again. These visits are called post-placement visits and serve to help you finalize your adoption. These visits will evaluate how life is going, how everyone is adjusting, and to complete required court reports that will be submitted with the request to finalize your adoption. This is an excellent time to ask about local support groups or play groups, or for additional resources regarding your unique adoption.

## Tips for the Home Study Visit

You will need to prepare for your home study and home visit by your social worker. Remember, social workers are doing a "people study," and part of that is to see where and how you live. They are not looking for a perfect model home, but one where a child will be safe and clean. You may wish to plan to have refreshments to offer your social worker so the appointment feels more like a visit and less like an interview.

Set the date and time for your visit and confirm the day before the appointment. If you have young children, be sure they are fed and rested prior to the visit, or even put them down for a nap before the appointed time. Be sure that you are also fed and rested, as the interview may be a few hours.

Clean and tidy your home the day before, picking up any items in your yard that are out of place. It doesn't have to be perfect, but presenting a home that is clean and neat is important. Your preparation is a good time to discover little changes or adaptations your home could use for a new child, such as minimizing clutter, reorganizing, or making your home more child friendly.

If you have pets, have them fed and put in their area to avoid distraction. They will need to be current on required vaccinations, and you may need to provide documentation as validation.

If you have been asked to complete or submit documents, be sure they are copied and clearly labeled. Similarly, if you have been given a list of topics that will be discussed, come prepared to the discussion. You will need to have ready answers to questions like: who will care for your child should something happen to you, how you plan to discipline your child, and other topics relating to parenting. If you are not a parent yet, these may not be topics you and your spouse have discussed, so some time spent in preparation may be well served.

When we were preparing for our first home study visit, I cleaned our condominium like I was expecting the queen! I was almost disappointed when our social worker didn't open the perfectly organized closets or check for dirt under the refrigerator. I had the house absolutely spotless, only to learn later that it wasn't a "white glove test" of our home.

One helpful thing we did to prepare for the interview was to casually discuss future decisions we'd have to make. We talked about childcare while we took our evening walk. We discussed child-rearing over dinner. We didn't stress about it, but rather, took time to come together about how we wanted to raise our family. If you haven't given these topics a lot of thought, don't worry. No one expects you to have all the answers, but it is a good opportunity to begin to prepare for parenthood.

## Adoption Profiles

You may be asked to prepare adoption profiles to be presented to potential birth mothers. They may also be referred to as lifebooks, Dear Birth Mother letters, or adoption resumes. Different adoption professionals may have individual requirements and requests, but most profiles contain some type of letter from you to the birth mother, describing your life as a prospective adoptive parent. Similarly, different professionals will provide different levels of service regarding profiles.

At our center, we assist adoptive families in preparing their adoption profiles by providing samples of successful profiles and one-on-one profile review services. It can be a difficult task to present your family in just the right way, so we take each family by the hand and guide them through the process. Because of our constant contact and interaction with birth parents, we understand what they are looking for as they consider adoptive family profiles. This allows us to work with each family individually to ensure that they are bringing out the uniqueness of their family in a way that will give a birth mother a reason to choose that family.

Before you put pencil to paper, do what professional writers do first: picture your reader in your mind. Ask yourself: *What does my birth parent want to know?* She wants to know what kind of parents you will be. She wants to imagine her baby growing up in a safe, loving home, having fun and getting help with homework. Be yourself and don't exaggerate or make up anything. God made you unique. Bring out the special qualities you have to offer as a parent.

The birth mothers I have worked with are far more interested in where you are going than where you have been. Share your hopes and dreams, the family goals you share, and your reason for pursuing adoption. Share what is unique about your family and the life you have to offer a child.

## WHAT MAKES YOU UNIQUE?

Mona and Dan lived in the High Desert of Nevada with their son, Jake, who was four years old. They had adopted him through a state agency two years before and wanted to adopt again, so they called me.

Full-figured with her short, strawberry blonde hair, Mona was outgoing and had a great smile. Dan was slender and handsome but, unlike his wife, was quiet and shy. Both were in their early thirties. Dan worked as a mechanic; Mona was a stay-at-home mom.

Our center started working on their profile. One photograph for the web page showed them standing with Jake in front of their neat doublewide modular home, surrounded by sand, sagebrush, and cactus. I got to know them pretty well. They lived a simple and unhurried life centered on their home and family. They rarely went on vacation trips, and their extended family consisted of some friends who lived hundreds of miles away.

Mona and Dan worried that their profile wouldn't stack up to those they'd seen of other adopting parents who had college degrees, a lot of money, big houses and lawns, grandparents nearby, and Hawaiian vacations planned.

I asked Dan if there was anything special about Mona.

"There is one thing," he said. "She's famous for her chocolate chip cookies. They're made from a secret recipe."

In the profile, we wrote that her cookies were the "best around those parts." One month later, Mona and Dan were chosen by a pregnant birth mother named Sarah, who told me that the cookies were the thing that had first appealed to her. She imagined her child coming home from school to chocolate chip cookies fresh from the oven, then climbing into Mona's soft lap to cuddle.

Around the office, Mona is remembered as our Chocolate Chip Cookie Mom. And I've got to tell you, hers were the best cookies I ever tasted, though she never would give me the recipe.

As Christians, we want to shout our faith to the world! When it comes to adoption profiles, birth mothers do want to know how your faith plays a role in your life, but keep it brief. There is a fine line between sharing your faith as a part of your life as prospective parents and sharing your faith in a way which may make her feel judged because of her current situation. Women in crisis relate to God differently, and many are afraid the reasons leading them to adoption mean God would not approve of them. You and I know God's love reaches out for her, but sometimes her perspective may keep her from seeing that now. Share your faith and how it will be a part of her child's life, but keep it in perspective.

*"Be wise in the way you act toward outsiders; make the most of every
opportunity. Let your conversation be always full of grace, seasoned
with salt, so that you may know how to answer everyone."*
Colossians 4:5,6

## Answering Your Questions

*What does an agency, attorney, and adoption facilitator do? And what do I
need?*

Their roles vary, and their expertise is essential to your success. Which
professional you select will depend on several factors, including the type of child
you seek, your expectations, and the method of adoption you use.

If you plan to adopt a newborn through an open, independent adoption, in
most states, you can choose a full-service licensed facilitator who will locate and
match you with a birth mother. They should also connect you to and work
closely with a qualified attorney. Many adoptive families find this to be the
preferable option because of the opportunity for nationwide exposure to birth
mothers.

An adoption agency can help with the entire process, however, the wait is
often longer due to the focus on birth mothers within their state lines and the
time spent providing home study and legal services for adoptive families. Be
sure to ask about potential wait times and the number of adoptions completed
per year through your local office.

Adoption attorneys will be required for the legal aspect of your adoption
and will be retained by you for an independent adoption, or provided for you as
part of the agency services if your birth mother is in your state. Get referrals for
attorneys when the time comes that you need one and be sure their specialty is
adoption.

*How do I know if the adoption facilitator I'm considering is properly
licensed or regulated?*

Many states don't regulate or require adoption facilitators to be licensed.
However, in the State of California adoption facilitators are regulated and
licensed. It should be as easy as asking your professional for their accreditations
with the state.

At our center, Lifetime Adoption, we are even able to work nationwide with
adoptive families and birth mothers who live outside of our state.

*Does the number of waiting families reflect how long I should expect to
wait for a match?*

No, this factor alone should not. You need to learn about a combination of
things, including the number of birth mothers they work with, the average wait
time, and other factors about the particular professional.

45

Your own adoption preferences and needs for your adoption will contribute to your wait, but the experience and statistics of the professional will influence your wait, as well.

Some professionals may only complete 6 adoptions per year, so if they have 40 waiting families, there may be cause for concern. At Lifetime Adoption, we complete over 120 adoptions per year, so over 120 waiting families are needed so birth mothers have a choice of families.

*Do adoption professionals provide the opportunity to speak with former clients?*

Yes, they should. And you should take the opportunity to contact the adoptive families and learn from them. Ask about the professional, but also ask about their adoption journey. This is a valuable opportunity to learn from others who have traveled the path you are considering.

Remember, these are people who are now parents, so they may not respond right away, so give them a little grace in awaiting a response. You should always ask for references.

*Can I adopt if I'm single? Can I adopt if I'm an older parent?*

Different adoption professionals have varying requirements for adoptive parents. The type of adoption you desire may also determine if you qualify as a single or older parent. At our center, we have assisted single women to adopt and have worked with adoptive parents from 21 to 60! There are many aspects adoption professionals generally consider when accepting prospective adoptive families, most of which consider the criteria birth parents are seeking in families to adopt their child.

Your adoption professional and home study provider can help you prepare for or consider issues you may face as a single or older parent.

## ADOPTION WISDOM

*"Let the word of Christ dwell in you richly as you teach and admonish one another with all wisdom, and as you sing psalms, hymns and spiritual songs with gratitude in your hearts to God."*
**Colossians 3:16**

Remember to spend time in the word daily. Spend time with other Christians. Ask for prayer. Ask for help. You are entering a phase of your adoption where the decisions you make will be affecting your journey. Take the time you need to feel confident you are following God's calling for you.

CHAPTER FOUR

# FUNDING YOUR ADOPTION

*"By wisdom a house is built, and through understanding it is established;*
*through knowledge its rooms are filled with rare and beautiful treasures."*
Proverbs 24: 3,4

Your family is the most important thing you will ever build, yet some families put more thought into their new car or home remodel than they do their adoption. You may have to budget, save, or even finance your adoption, but the value of your investment, a life enriched by a child, can never be measured!

Before agreeing to work with any adoption professional, ask for their contract, fee schedule, and outline of anticipated additional costs to complete your adoption. If the organization mentions "match" or "placement" fees, be sure to ask what happens if the match or placement fails. Be sure to get everything in writing.

## How Much does it Cost to Adopt?

- Fees for public agency or foster adoptions of special needs and older children range from no cost to $5,500.
- Some private agencies offer sliding-scale fees based on income; however, these are becoming less common.
- Domestic private agency adoptions are expensive and can run to more than $40,000.
- Independent adoptions, arranged through an attorney or licensed facilitator, are usually less expensive, averaging $15,000 to $25,000.
- International adoption, through private agencies, runs $15,000 to $45,000, plus additional costs for such items as medical exams and travel or an escort to bring your child home, depending on the country's requirements.

## Adoption Agency Fees

If you are completing your adoption through an agency, you will find fees from $20,000 to $35,000 and up, depending on your state of residence and the extent of services offered. Some agencies offer a flat fee and a few have a sliding scale based on your income. Ask if you will need to hire an attorney for the birth parents' termination of rights or if that's included in the fee.

Your agency fee typically provides services to locate birth mothers and children and counseling and support for birth mothers and adoptive parents. It also may include parenting classes, birth mother expenses, including prenatal and delivery care, if not paid by insurance, post-placement visits and the finalization report for the court.

Currently, many agencies are downsizing the services they provide for domestic adoption and shifting their focus to international adoption. Be sure to ask for a current list of services included with the program in which you are interested.

## Adoption Facilitation Fees

Most states allow families to use a licensed adoption facilitator in lieu of an adoption agency. In fact, California now regulates this practice and maintains a list of qualified adoption facilitators. The advantages of using a qualified and experienced adoption facilitator are that families typically adopt sooner, with less expense, and more control. Many facilitators work hand-in-hand with adoption attorneys and adoption home study providers nationwide to help complete the adoption.

Adoption facilitation fees are typically $12,000 to $25,000, but may include nationwide birth mother outreach, whereas adoption agencies are often limited by the borders of their state.

The practice of adopting outside your own state, called interstate adoption, is very attractive to families who live in states where the legal aspect of adoption is restrictive and outdated. Many attorneys utilize state laws in Texas, Kansas, and California to legally allow non-residents to use their laws when finalizing adoptions, resulting in the rise of adoptive families using adoption facilitators to help build their families.

If you choose a licensed adoption facilitator, ensure you are choosing one who works directly with birth mothers, and not just a referral or consulting service that adds another layer of fees onto other organizations' available adoption situations. This adds unnecessary costs to your adoption. At our center, we only work with our own birth mothers and adoptive families nationwide and do not make our adoption situations available for other consultants to "shop around."

# Public Agency Fees

To some families, adopting an infant is not a priority. By choosing an older child who is waiting for a loving home, they can save a lot of money. The adoption itself, through a state agency or licensed private agency, can be free or very reasonable. The agency may take payments, and you may receive a reimbursement of adoption costs through programs that provide incentives for parents to provide permanency to children in foster care and adoption subsidies. These older children usually have special needs or are in sibling groups of multi-ethnic heritage.

### COST FACTORS IN ADOPTION

- A typical U.S. adoption costs between $12,500 and $55,000.
- Federal adoption tax credits can reduce your costs by over $13,000.
- Your employer may provide adoption benefits. The benefits usually run from $1,000 to $12,000.
- Government subsidies can reduce the cost of special needs adoptions to little or nothing.
- With an independent or private adoption, you can save money by choosing only the services and professionals you need.

## Home Study Fees

Home study fees can vary considerably, depending on the state where you live. A home study for independent adoption is normally less than one for an agency adoption and averages about $2,000 across the United States. Some states, like Texas, have more affordable home studies, while New England states often run higher than the average.

Most state or public adoption agencies charge a reduced or no-cost home study if you adopt a waiting child through their program. Some states allow private social workers, rather than social service department employees, to do home studies for non-agency adoptions. Many states offer home study services through their social service departments.

## Interstate Adoption Costs

If you adopt from another state, you will need to have an adoption professional, an attorney, an agency, or in some states, a licensed social worker to take the birth parents' signatures. Your home state adoption attorney will normally coordinate paperwork for the Interstate Compact. Be aware that some agencies will charge a few thousand dollars just to take birth mother, and in some cases birth father, signatures and mail them to your agency in your state.

## Adoption Fee Guide

- Compare fees and services of adoption professionals you are considering, as they may vary.
- Clarify up front and in writing exactly what services the stated adoption fees will and will not cover.
- Some agencies may quote a fee, but later add charges for services like post-placement visits, travel, postage, or court costs. While these may be legitimate costs, it is your responsibility to be aware of them.
- Some professionals require the entire fee to be paid when services start. As soon as the contract is signed, they begin searching for your child. This is a common practice.
- Since you are paying for services and not for a baby (which is unlawful), use only reputable professionals and sign a contract that clearly specifies what you're paying for.
- The contract should also spell out your responsibilities.
- Be wary of any adoption professional who will accept you as a client without first reviewing your application or a home study.
- Not all organizations with Christian names are Christian based. Ask for a statement of faith and decide on an organization because of their reputation.
- Be cautious of adoption professionals who ask for payment only when they have a match for you. This practice is often a sign that the professional doesn't complete many adoptions or that he has no obligation to actively seek an adoption for you.

## Tips for Keeping Track of Your Adoption Expenses

Develop a budget for your expenses. Once you begin to do this, it will make tax time so much easier. You can use a program like QuickBooks, one of the financial software programs that come with your computer, or even an old-fashioned ledger book.

So many expenses involved in adopting are deductible, but they are deductible only if you take advantage of them. Believe me, the government is not going to tell you if you have forgotten a deduction. Check with your accountant, as well. Make sure your tax preparer is aware that you are adopting so he can assist you in your tax preparation. (See Resources in the back of this book.)

## Things to Remember When Budgeting

- Use an accounting program, if at all possible.
- Balance your checkbook each month. Having accurate totals will help ease your adoption stress.

- Watch your ATM usage—even though they're so easy to use and so convenient!
- Do you really need a big screen TV, new furniture, or a latte every morning? Be thoughtful and reasonable with your spending.
- Stick to the necessities until your adoption is final.
- Discover the difference between what you need and what you want!
- Always ask for receipts to add to your growing file of deductible expenses.

## Adoption Tax Credit

The good news is that you may qualify for a federal tax credit of over $13,000 for qualified expenses to adopt a qualifying baby or child. At times, the credit may also be allowed for a special needs adoption, even when there are no qualified expenses for the adoption. Currently, there are limits to this credit if your modified gross income is over $182,000, but check with your tax consultant for current IRS statutes.

### WHICH EXPENSES QUALIFY FOR THE TAX CREDIT?

Most legally allowed adoption expenses qualify for the credit, including:
- Fees paid to adoption agency and licensed adoption facilitator.
- Court costs and interstate compact fees.
- Attorney and/or adoption service provider fees.
- Travel expenses, including meals and lodging.

Certain expenses are specifically not allowed such as:
- Fees that violate state or federal law.
- Fees paid to arrange surrogate parenting.
- Expenses for adopting a spouse's child.
- Employer paid or reimbursed adoption fees.
- Fees paid before 1997.

Generally speaking, once the adoption is final, you are able to apply for and take the federal tax credit. It is encouraging that the credit may also be available to help offset money lost in a failed adoption attempt. Please refer all tax planning questions to your CPA, who will have the most current IRS regulations and can apply them to your specific financial situation.

## Birth Mother Expenses

Some birth mothers may have health insurance, jobs, and a place to stay during their pregnancy. They may need no financial assistance from you. Others may need help.

In many states, you can assist a birth mother during her pregnancy for food, rent, medical care, counseling and other expenses, such as maternity clothes, gas, and travel expenses. Always check with a qualified adoption attorney because laws vary greatly. In my experience, I have found about half of all birth mothers do ask for help. Some may need help as little as $100, but many birth mothers who need assistance will average about $2,000.

When you become matched with a birth mother, you will usually place a budgeted amount into a trust fund with your attorney for your birth mother's expenses. The attorney will disperse the expenses as needed, often directly toward the specific need, such as the landlord, doctor's office, or phone company. Such payments are considered gifts, and if the adoption is not completed, birth parents are not required to repay them by law. Laws vary from state to state, and using a qualified adoption attorney is an absolute necessity.

## How Can We Make Adoption Affordable?

Many families experience sticker shock after looking into adoption and stop right there. Yet many people make monthly payments for a car or even a home remodel. Your car may only last ten years, but your family is for a lifetime! Your first step in affording adoption may be reprioritizing your current expenses.

### Planning Ahead

Monica and her husband contacted our center about adopting again. They had adopted previously but were excited to get started right away for their next child. We knew that it had been a struggle financially the first time, so we gently asked about their budget this time.

Monica shared that they had researched the companies with the best adoption benefits and targeted them in their job search efforts after her husband had been laid off. It paid off, and he was now working for a company that offered an $8,000 adoption benefit!

You should ask your employer or human resources department about any adoption benefits that may be available. Many employers are now including this as part of their benefit packages. Similarly, consult your health insurance carrier. Some insurance allows a one-time infertility *or* adoption benefit that may be available for you.

Learn about the federal adoption tax credit and any state tax credit available for you. This may be the best way to reimburse some of your adoption expenses. Talk to your CPA or tax preparer if you have additional questions.

There may be adoption grants out there, but be aware there are many more applicants than there are grants. Time spent completing applications may be better used pursuing funds directly for your adoption, such as garage sales, online auctions, or a second job.

Consider also your financing options, including a home equity loan or financing via low- or no-interest credit cards. Borrowing against a 401k is also a feasible option. Financing options have helped thousands of families adopt successfully.

Talk to your family, as well. Often, friends and family members are willing to help when they know their funds are going directly to help a child in their own family.

## Get Creative!

It helps to think of adoption in the same perspective as other financial investments. For instance, a couple may buy a new boat on credit, but are hesitant to finance an adoption. They may need to ask themselves, "What is my priority right now?" Is it a boat for occasional summer weekends or a family for a lifetime?

This is where it's time to get serious and get creative about what you want and how to get there. Here are some ideas to get you started:

- Do you get a latte and bagel every morning? Some people spend $6 a morning on something they could do at home for under $1. That savings of $5 a day amounts to over $1,200 per year! And if both husband and wife make that change, it's over $2,400 savings annually!
- Similarly, are you dining out for lunch? Whether it's the bargain menu at fast food or a sit-down restaurant, is there money you could save at lunch time and put toward an adoption? And what about dinners out? If it's more than twice a week, there's likely some savings that could happen there, too. This could be thousands of dollars!
- Look around your house and your garage. Do you have things that could be treasures to someone else? Is it time to cut the clutter? Consider a garage sale for fundraising. Ask a couple friends to contribute, too. A good garage sale can net over $1,000 in a day! And don't limit it to just one sale, ask a few other friends and have another one. Offer to help them clean out their garage or cupboards in exchange for the stuff they opt to get rid of and sell.
- Do you have time for a second job? Realistically look at your budget and your time. You may be able to take a few extra hours for a few months to build up your savings for adoption, even if it is taking on something as basic as mowing a few lawns or cleaning houses.
- What about your skills and talents? Do you do something that could be a blessing to others? If you are a teacher, perhaps you could get a few tutoring clients on the weekend. If you play the piano, perhaps you could offer lessons or to play for parties. Even something as simple as organizing can be a skill someone would be happy to pay you for!

- Be cautious about "selling" products to raise money. I have seen many families try to sell candy, candles, make-up, and kitchen utensils in an attempt to fundraise. Remember that many people are already overwhelmed with these types of fundraising requests from schools, churches, and other organizations, and it may not yield the most help for your immediate adoption funds.
- Talk about your goals, write them down, and tell others. Sometimes help and assistance come from the most unlikely sources. Commit them also to God. If this is His will for you, He will help provide the resources you need.
- Plan a fundraiser, such as an evening for families in your church or neighborhood. A spaghetti feed in the church social hall, a local band to provide music in exchange for the exposure, and a silent auction of donations from friends could help you reach your financial goals quickly through this adoption fundraiser evening. Friends and family members are likely eager to help. Or enlist a local Boy or Girl Scout troop to help. This provides a wholesome family event for the community, too!

## Adoption IS Possible!

Todd and Shylin hoped to adopt a newborn infant, but their monthly income just covered their monthly expenses. They really thought adoption was hopeless until they started making some difficult decisions.

First to go was Todd's car, a newer model SUV. It not only had a hefty payment, but sizable gas consumption and insurance payment. He bought a bicycle instead for his daily commute. It was a sudden and huge monthly increase in their savings!

About a month into Todd's new commute, he realized a side effect he didn't expect: his health was improving! He gave up his monthly gym membership (that he wasn't using much anyway) and found more monthly savings. Rather than movies and dining out on the weekends, they began to hike as a couple together with a packed lunch. They traded their pricey tropical vacation plans for a week trekking part of the Pacific Crest Trail together.

As Todd got healthier, he found himself more motivated to become an active father in a child's life. Their combined passion toward adoption was increasing, and they found more ways to save money to begin the family of their dreams. Within nine months, they had their entire adoption budget saved and, as an added bonus, were both in the best shape of their lives!

With effort, ingenuity, and planning you, too, will find a way to pursue the adoption of your heart's desire.

## Answering Your Questions

*Are there grants available for families who are wanting to adopt but can't afford to?*

Yes, there are some grants available, but they are extremely limited in nature. There are far more families applying than there are funds available.

The best advice I can give to families who are hoping to secure grant funds is to instead research the tax credit, employer benefits, and ways they can raise money for their own adoption.

One grant that is consistently available to qualified parents is the African American Enrichment Grant through Lifetime Adoption Foundation. Currently it is offering grants of over $4,000 to qualified families. You can learn more at www.AAAdoptions.com.

*We just want to provide a loving, Christian home for a child in need. Why does it have to cost so much?*

As with fertility treatments or other services, there are costs to adoption. We don't go into a doctor and suggest that they should care for people only out of kindness; we understand that they must cover the costs of the care they provide. Those who provide adoption services must also pay for electricity, phones, computers, employees, and a location.

Even free or low-cost adoptions are not free. They are paid for by millions of tax dollars. Right now, as government services are cash-strapped, many subsidized-agencies are not providing the services that women and children need in many parts of the country. Private adoption organizations and some non-profit organizations are stepping in to provide care that these people so desperately need.

If cost is a factor, consider private or independent adoptions where you can hand-select the professionals you use to keep costs lower. You need to only employ the professionals and services that you need, rather than selecting a full-service organization that may include services you won't need.

## ADOPTION WISDOM

*"Do not be anxious about anything, but in everything, by prayer and petitions, with thanksgiving, present your requests to God."*
**Philippians 4:6**

Step by step, task by task, day by day, you are being led by Him. Don't let finances stop you from finding the child God has meant for you. If He has provided the desire, He will provide the means, as well.

# CHAPTER FIVE

# TRUST THE CALL

*"Finally, brothers, whatever is true, whatever is noble, whatever is right, whatever is pure, whatever is lovely, whatever is admirable—if anything is excellent or praiseworthy—think about such things."*
Philippians 4:8

An important distinction of people who succeed at adoption is that they have faith in their desires, are very intentional in their steps, and are focused on their goal. Many prospective adoptive parents look and dream about adopting but do little to move past that point. While it is wise to do research before moving on to adopt, there are many who don't move any further to complete what they have started. Sadly, fear is often the culprit. You have to believe you will adopt!

Many years ago, I was caring for a baby who was going to be adopted. I had him in my arms and was standing outside my church after services when Grace, a woman I knew, came up to me. She was spry and cheerful at the age of 82, and she looked at the child with shining eyes.

"Babies are so wonderful," she said. She was quiet for a time. "I wish I had known you when I was younger. I would have asked you to find a baby for me to adopt." It turned out she and her husband were unable to have children.

Grace was a loving person who was always around children, so I had assumed she was a mother. But on that Sunday morning, I learned she had lived her whole life without the joy of sharing her love with a son or daughter.

"We didn't know what to do or where to begin," she said. "So we never did have a baby." If only someone long ago had helped her get started on the road to adoption, she would have had her little one.

If, like Grace, you are unable to have a biological child or have always wanted to adopt and with all your heart you want to love, nurture, and bring up a child, then you should set out to find the child meant for you.

Successful adoptive parents know that the timing, planning, and dedication to completing their adoption goal can make its success much easier and smoother. I believe with any goal, there are basic steps that must be taken to attain the desired end result... becoming a parent! Those who have gone before you know it takes time and patience and following a concise plan to realize adoption success.

I do believe the Lord doesn't allow us more than we can handle and that even the obstacles or the birth mothers who change their mind are part of His plan, too. I can't imagine not having my son, and I wouldn't if it weren't for the birth mother who changed her mind before I met his birth mother. Thank God He has a plan!

*"Be strong and courageous. Do not be afraid or terrified because of them,*
*for the Lord your God goes with you;*
*He will never leave you nor forsake you."*
Deuteronomy 31:6

## Paperwork, Paperwork, Paperwork...

Adoption requires a lot of information in the form of paperwork and personal information. Sharpen your pencil and dig in! You will need patience with the process and perseverance with the process to be successful.

If at any point you find things overwhelming, work an hour or two a day on your adoption, then put it away. By doing this, your paperwork can still be done in a timely manner and you are not overwhelmed with a mountain of questions.

My best advice for this stage of your adoption is to just get it done. Without the completed paperwork, an adoption cannot take place. Approach this with the priority it deserves and spend time getting things done. These are the steps I took when adopting, and most every other adoptive parent has taken them, too. I worked one hour a day on my adoption, and then I put it away. Pray over your work and leave it in His hands.

## Tips for Being Successful in Adoption

- Learn all you can from current books and the Internet about adoption and parenting.
- Write out a clear and logical adoption plan: Decide which type of adoption is best. Review and revise your plan as you pursue your goal to adopt.
- Be realistic and honest when you evaluate your finances and work out your adoption budget.
- Be diligent in taking care of each step your adoption professional asks you to do in a timely manner.

- Assess your emotional readiness to adopt, as well as that of your family.
- This can be a stressful time in your home. Don't neglect your marriage or other children as you work toward your adoption.
- Be patient, remembering that it takes nine months to have a baby biologically and your adoptive child may not even be conceived yet!
- Be prepared for the process to take several years if your specific requirements for a child are narrow.
- Get involved with other adopting families for emotional support and to enhance your parenting skills and the quality of your adoption experience.
- To relieve stress and stay focused, visualize holding your child in your arms. Believe it will happen!
- Know that adopting is like being pregnant. A wife may experience hormonal changes, and both partners may experience fear, excitement, and even sleepless nights.
- Lean on each other and share the vision of your child. Your love will grow as you work and pray together to realize your dream.
- Pray together for adoption.

In the many years I've worked helping families adopt, there are a few things I tell my clients they must have to be successful with our center. I'll share them with you, too:

1. Plenty of adoption profiles, so birth mothers can see you.
2. Contact numbers, so you can be reached.
3. A true desire to adopt a child and the ability to love a child not of your body, but of your heart.
4. Accurate preferences, meaning you are ready to say yes to a child within your stated adoption requirements.
5. Being all 'prayed up'! You may not have more than a short period of time to consider a match. If your walk with the Lord is in order, you will be prepared to pursue the adoption He has waiting.

## Remember, Your Adoption in His Timing

Have you ever looked at another person and thought, "Has she got it made! God has really blessed her!"

She has what you want—a child to call her own, maybe great parents, a strong marriage, a spouse who loves Jesus. Maybe you envy her successful professional life, the ease of getting pregnant or adopting, or material blessings that have not kept them from loving Jesus.

Sometimes we look at the blessings from God in another person's life with a longing to experience the same goodness. We find ourselves fighting feelings of envy or possibly even disappointment with God because we didn't get what we consider necessary for our happiness, such a child, either biological or through adoption.

Until you make Christ the center of your life, my friend, you'll never be satisfied or fulfilled. Remember Jesus' words to Peter when the fisherman wanted to know His plans for another disciple? *Jesus answered, "If I want him to remain alive until I return, what is that to you? You must follow me."* (John 21:22)

Do not worry or concern yourself with what God has done in His timing in someone else's life. You will only miss out on the blessing God has for you. In His timing, He will bless you, too, in the perfect way that is best for you with the child He has for just you.

## Answering Your Questions

*We are so scared about the adoption process that we have been putting off starting. I don't know why. What should I do?*

I can share with you from my own adoption journey that many of us feel scared, doubtful, abandoned, and unsure on what to do, and we sometimes feel just plain stuck. If I were sitting across from you, I would ask you directly, "Where do you think this fear comes from? Who do you think wants to prevent you from moving forward and adopting?" I think the enemy is trying his hardest to prevent wonderful and loving people from becoming Christian parents. Don't let him win!

Start taking steps today if you truly want to become parents through adoption. The Lord knows the desires of your heart. He will hold your hand and guide you if you take time to listen.

*We finally completed the paperwork, YAY! But now we feel a bit lost. It took so much work to get the home study and profile prepared, I feel like everything has come to a halt now that we are waiting. Is this normal?*

Yes, it is quite common, especially because the waiting is what often characterizes the most difficult part of the adoption, and the part in which you have the least control. However, now is not when you should be just biding your time. There are a lot of things you can be doing right now to prepare for "the call" (See Chapter 7, Your Adoption Journey).

It might feel like there is an endless amount of work with the early steps to adoption, only to drop off to nearly nothing for a long while. Don't fall into the trap of feeling as though there is nothing to do. This is a time of preparation, use it wisely.

# ADOPTION WISDOM

*"Be still and know that I am God."*
**Psalm 46:10**

Remember to take time to be quiet, to reflect on your adoption journey.
Acknowledge God is in control and capable of fulfilling your desires.
These are the moments you will hear Him leading.

CHAPTER SIX

# YOUR CHILD'S BIRTH FAMILY

*"In love He predestined us to be adopted as His sons through Jesus Christ,*
*in accordance with His pleasure and will —*
*to the praise of His glorious grace,*
*which He has freely given us in the One He loves."*
Ephesians 1: 5,6

Often in adoption, you will hear the phrase "adoption triad." The adoption triad is made up of the adoptive parents, the birth parents, and the child. Depending on the situation, there may be little or no involvement by the birth parents. However, it bears remembering that regardless of your knowledge of the birth family, they will be a very real part of your child's life, even if completely absent or unknown.

## Talking About Adoption

Beginning the day your child joins your family, actively explaining the love of adoption will help with their adjustment and a positive self-image. People often ask me about when I told my children about adoption. The first day I pinched my son's little cheeks, I told him, "I'm so glad your birth mother chose me!"

Recently, my son, who now towers above me, shared with me how grateful he was that I have always been so open about his adoption. "I'm so glad you didn't wait to tell me I was adopted," he said. "I can't imagine finding out at 10 or 12 years old. That would have been a disaster!" For me, this is a testimony to the power of loving honesty when talking about adoption.

It is not required that you share all the details of a difficult or immoral lifestyle, but focusing on the choice made in love will do much to help your child see their adoption for the gift that it is. There are many wonderful books that can help explain adoption to children of any age, even some written toward adoption in specific countries!

If you are adopting internationally, there likely will be little information available. You can request (and even require!) the most recent medical records on your child. Typically, orphanages and foster homes will provide all they have, but you should expect very little information, and be grateful if there is more.

For example, one couple who adopted from China has a scrap of paper with their child's birth date on it, which was pinned to her clothing when she was abandoned at the orphanage. That is all they know about her life prior to that day.

Share the information you have, and fill in the blanks with the typical lifestyle and customs of her country. There are many ways to do this.

> **Helpful Tip:**
> Make a color copy of any scrapbook or lifebook you make so your child has one to frequently look at or take to school, so the original one is always in a safe place.

One common way families share and communicate about international adoption is to create a lifebook. Scrapbooking is a wonderful way to preserve the information you have and share the journey you made. For instance, photograph the orphanage, the staff, the foster family, even her bed! Take pictures of your time together in those first days; note everything you were told about her and take pictures of the city. All of these facts and photos can create the scrapbook that begins her life.

In a domestic adoption, a birth mother usually plays an active role in her child's adoption. An independent adoption will typically provide much information, as well as the opportunity for acquiring even more directly from the birth parents.

As your child grows, regardless of how much or how little you know about your child's birth family, remember to keep them in prayer, and even pray for them with your child. The decision they made was a difficult one, and prayer may be all you can offer them. Providing your child with the information now, from an early age, will help them as they grow, develop, and question their own life and purpose.

## SHE NEEDS YOUR PRAYERS

*Be a Prayer Warrior for a Birth Mother!*

*What if you are the only one who ever prayed for your birth mother?*

*You may be part of God's plan for her.*

# A 'Good' Adoption Match

Whether you are waiting to be chosen by a birth mother, or waiting for your international match to come through, understanding that God's hand is at work will help prepare your heart.

When evaluating an adoption match, your emotions should not be the driving force in accepting it. This is sometimes easier said than done. Ask the questions, wait for answers, and be realistic in your decision. I've heard families debate about whether "the next match" might be better, but I can assure you that far too often, "the next match" doesn't arrive for months or even years. You may not get an unlimited number of adoption situations to consider, so be in tune with God's leading. Remember He will not allow you more than you can handle.

In a match for a domestic adoption, the mutual agreement to move forward will be between the adoptive parents and the birth mother. For international adoption, it will need to be a mutual agreement between the adoptive mother and adoptive father, after discussing the facts they have about the child with their pediatrician.

There is no official checklist of items to define a good match, but rather it is the mutual agreement to move forward with an adoption in the best interest of the child.

> ### Be Yourself
> Leah and Mike were a sweet, Christian couple in their 40's, who had been waiting longer than most to adopt. They were faithful and patient, yet just never seemed to garner a birth mother's attention. Their physical appearance was a bit outdated, and their Washington home was quite plain. After over two years of waiting, they were selected by a woman who was having boy/girl twins. Needless to say, our staff was delighted!
>
> The adoption went very smoothly, and later, when we received pictures of both the birth mother and the adoptive parents, we could see exactly why this birth mother chose them. Her look was outdated, just like them! She likely chose them because they seemed to have something in common physically, and she knew she wouldn't be judged.
>
> Sure enough, now six years later, the twins looked exactly like them all. It was truly a match made in heaven!

Here are three things you should know before accepting a match:

- You can accept the situation as presented to you today. You may never have more answers to your questions.
- Understand that no situation will seem perfect. Passing on a situation will create a family for someone else, and you may continue with an even longer wait.
- Be sure that your home study is complete and you are able to move forward financially.

# Fear of the Unknown

In adoption, as with life, there are no guarantees. God instructs us to "not worry about tomorrow, for tomorrow will worry about itself." (Matthew 6:34) He promises that if we "seek first His kingdom and His righteousness, all these things will be given to you." (Matthew 6:33).

Prepare yourself to accept unknown factors in your adoption, for there will likely be some questions for which you will never receive answers. For instance, your child's birth father may be completely unknown, the pregnancy a result of rape or a one-night-stand. You may receive nothing more than the very basic information about a child in an orphanage; even the child's birth date may be unknown. You need to prepare yourself to accept what you can live with and let go of the need to control and understand every detail.

If you find yourself challenged at this step, it may be good to revisit the original motivation for adoption. Do you really want to be a parent, or are you looking for a perfect situation?

Many years ago, I worked with a couple, Maggie and Ron, who were chosen six different times by a birth mother. Each time, they found a different reason to decline the match. One time it was due to the lack of birth father medical records (something that rarely is provided), another time they stated they were uncomfortable because the birth mother was concealing her pregnancy from her mother, and the last time it was just "a feeling." It was clear that no matter what the situation, they just were not prepared to say yes. In the end, while I was saddened that they chose to remain childless rather than take a risk with adopting a child, perhaps it was a blessing that a child was not placed in a home where perfection seemed to be a prerequisite.

The lesson here is that we must be prepared. Taking the time to learn how adoption works and what to expect might have prepared this couple to say yes, or it may have dissuaded them from ever beginning the process in the first place. Either way, preparation is always key, even if only to prepare for a leap of faith.

# Answering Your Questions

*What should I expect to receive from my birth mother?*

In a domestic adoption, medical records are typically available from a birth mother, depending on the level of prenatal care. Limited information may be available for the birth father, however, medical records usually are not.

You should expect (and receive) honesty from your birth mother and in turn be honest with her. Most women are honest about their use of substances during pregnancy, as well as their medical history. Adoptive parents should always be honest about their commitment to ongoing contact after the adoption.

Your birth mother may have the same values as you do, however, she may have gotten off track. She may have made poor decisions or been abandoned by the man in her life. Her upbringing may be similar to yours or it may be vastly different. Try not to go into a situation with a preconceived notion of what she will be like – it is likely you will be very surprised.

It is important to remember that birth mothers typically live a different lifestyle and are not on the same time schedule we are. Their priorities may be very different and likely affected by the hormonal changes normal with pregnancy.

You should expect that your birth mother may be quite different than you. She may have tattoos, piercings, and purple hair, but that doesn't mean she doesn't love her child and want the best for him. That doesn't mean she isn't any less one of God's children than we all are.

> **Reflect God's Grace**
> Have grace with your birth mother, just as God has grace with us. Her choices may be different from yours, but the gift she offers is priceless.

*"For it is by grace you have been saved, through faith—*
*and this is not from yourselves; it is the gift of God."*
Ephesians 2:8

*Will we be able to name or rename our child? What if the birth mother wants to name him?*

If you are matched with a pregnant woman, she will have the opportunity to name her baby, and this name will show on the original birth certificate. When the birth certificate is reissued after your adoption is finalized, it will show you as parents and whatever name you have chosen.

If your birth mother wants to name her child and asks you to retain the name, honor your commitment if you agree to do so or try to reach a compromise. For example, you may wish to retain the name she has chosen as a middle name.

I always encourage families to not make the name a deal-breaker. In my own adoption, part of the agreement with our birth mother was to keep the name she had given him. It may not have been my choice, but I loved it because I loved him.

If you adopt an older child, seek professional advice when considering a name change. Some parents involve the child in the discussion if he or she is old enough. Others simply begin by calling a toddler something different. This can cause identity issues. If you do decide to change your child's name, consider doing it slowly or calling him by two names for a while.

For example, Sheila adopted Carl from foster care when he was nearly 18 months old. He had the same first name as his birth father, who was in prison for killing Carl's mother. Sheila wanted to separate this sweet child from the identity of his father, so she began calling him Carl Jacob. Over time, she dropped Carl altogether, and he became simply Jacob. Legally, Carl is no longer part of his name.

## ADOPTION WISDOM

Believe. That's all we need to do. Yet some days it seems easier to believe we are hopeless than to believe in His promises.

*"Everything is possible for him who believes."*
**Mark 9:23**

Part of our walk with our Father is trust. We know He won't give us more difficulties than our strength through Him can sustain. We know He will not abandon us. We believe though we cannot see Him, we trust in His word, we trust in the heavenly kingdom He is preparing for us. I challenge you to give Him the same trust with your adoption journey.

CHAPTER SEVEN

# YOUR ADOPTION JOURNEY

*"For God did not give us a spirit of timidity, but a spirit of power."*
2 Timothy 1:7

Your adoption journey will be defined largely by the type of adoption you have chosen. While the journey may be different, there will be characteristics that they all share. While the choices you have made about the type of adoption to pursue will provide a framework for your journey, remember that every adoption is unique.

**International adoptions** are characterized by a great deal of paperwork and certifications that, when completed, are followed by a wait to be matched with your child. Because you know specifically the country you will adopt from, your wait time will likely give you ample opportunity to prepare and learn about the country.

Travel is typically required and may be for up to three weeks or more, with some countries requiring a minimum of two visits. Some organizations do not require both parents to travel internationally to adopt their child; however, I always recommend it. This will be an important aspect of your first days as a family.

While you are in another country, you may find the lack of organization, poor living conditions, and requests for bribes shocking, yet understand they are commonplace in some countries.

**Adopting domestically through the foster system** usually requires extensive classes and certifications, and may be followed by numerous temporary placements until the child that is ultimately meant for your family arrives. You may feel pressured to adopt a child who is outside of your adoption preferences or become weary of providing temporary care. Be certain of what is right for your family.

Looking into adoption of waiting children outside of your state is always a possibility, and, if you are open to older children and sibling groups, may be your best option when you are weary of waiting on a foster adoption to materialize.

**Independent or private agency domestic adoptions** allow adoptive families to have a little more control in the design of their own adoption journey. Choices can be made to limit the search geographically or be open to the entire U.S. Wait times can often be decreased if adoption preferences are widened. Additional adoption professionals may also be enlisted to supplement the search for your child.

Travel to the state of the child's residence or birth will be required and a stay of up to ten days prior to returning home, depending on the circumstances.

**Common to all paths is the wait.** Pregnancy takes nine months; adoption often takes longer. Readying yourself for the wait can be one of the biggest preparations you can make.

> ### Helpful Adoption Travel Tips
>
> - Be sure to mention that you are adopting. Some airlines and hotels offer special discounts.
>
> - Pay for travel cancellation insurance in case something unforeseen arises.
>
> - Look into surrounding airports when booking flights.
>
> - Register for miles, points, and anything else you can for each part of your journey.

*Don't run ahead of God's plan; don't be impatient in your wait. Enjoy the journey of adoption, of building your family, the family God has for you and the child that God has meant for your family.*

*"There is a time for everything, and a season for every activity under heaven."*
Ecclesiastes 3:1

## What to Do While You Wait

Rarely in life do happiness and fear mix as dramatically as during the time when adoptive parents are waiting for the birth of their child or for the adoption to become irrevocable. Similarly, waiting for a match or to be chosen can seem like an endless time. It can sometimes feel hopeless.

I'd like to share with you a few suggestions that I have found helpful, both emotionally and practically. Choose the ones that work best for you.

- Accept support from other adoptive parents who have walked the path before you. You can find them online and in your community. Ask your agency, attorney, or licensed facilitator for the names of other adoptive parents in your area. You will likely be surprised by how many people you know who are touched by adoption!

- Start shopping for age-appropriate items. Create a list and have fun buying the items for your future child.
- If you're adopting an infant, start thinking about names. Create a short list and finalize your selections.
- Read. Visit Amazon.com, ChristianBook.com, and other online sites for literature on child development or parenting subjects that you would like to know more about.
- Enroll in a class: CPR, parenting, or early childhood development. Make yourself feel comfortable and more prepared for your new role as an adoptive parent.
- If you will be hiring a nanny or using day care, investigate and narrow down your options. Make a plan.
- Determine whom you would like to name as your child's guardians and/or godparents. Be sure to discuss it with the individuals involved.
- Consider preparing your child's room. However, if you are adopting an older child, it's best to wait and let him or her make the decorating choices.
- Make a videotape as a future birthday gift for your child. Include your hopes and dreams as you wait, as well as messages from immediate family members about their eager anticipation.
- If you are adopting a waiting child, prepare a list of questions for your child's pre-adoption caregiver or foster mom so you have a better idea of the child's likes, dislikes, and behaviors.
- If you plan to travel to pick up your child, research hotels and airlines. If possible, book sufficiently in advance to take advantage of lower rates. Check online booking sources that often offer last-minute low rates.
- When making travel plans, arrive a day or two early, if possible. This will give you the opportunity to recover from jet lag, purchase any items you forgot, and acclimate yourself to your destination.
- If you are so moved, purchase small thank you gifts for the birth parents and various adoption professionals. However, consult first with your adoption attorney before giving a gift to the birth parents to avoid any misinterpretation by the courts. This may also be appropriate for the caregivers at the orphanage, foster parents, or host family.
- If you are adopting internationally, study your child's country of origin. Purchase travel videos and brochures, search the Internet, and educate yourself on the relevant customs, culture, and language. Try to learn a few words in your child's language. This can help you avoid embarrassing mistakes.

- Volunteer your time to non-profit organizations. Giving your talents to help others will relieve the anxiety associated with the wait and will bless others in need.

If you feel yourself struggling with the wait to adopt or find yourself struggling to stay hopeful that your dreams will be fulfilled, examine what choices you can consciously make to help you stay focused on God's promises.

If you have people in your life who are negative, limit your time with them. If you feel as though your life is on hold during the wait, make changes. Life goes on during our times of waiting for other things; it should go on during your adoption wait, as well. Take a class, plan a trip, learn a new skill, or treasure the time you have now, because once your child enters your world, life will never again be the same.

If you've taken the required steps and chosen experienced adoption professionals, now is the time to trust in your planning and release the worries and fears. God is in control.

## Planning for After the Adoption

Now is the time to prepare for the emotions and challenges that will accompany the joys and delights of parenthood through adoption. Here are a few important things you should do now to be ready for what the future holds:

### Pediatricians

Don't wait until your child is home to begin looking for a pediatrician. It will benefit your adoption if you have a doctor chosen before you are ever matched. In private and international adoption, many times case workers or hospitals will not release the child to you until you can put a pediatrician's name and contact information on file. In both situations, it can be helpful to have a pediatrician to help review any medical records.

- Make calls to your insurance provider to learn about the requirements and time frames for adding your child to your medical, dental, and other insurance plans. Review your life insurance, too, now that you are growing your family.

- If you will need childcare or to enroll an older child in school, begin your research, especially if you will need an English-as-a-second-language (ESL) program. Talk to other adoptive parents about their experiences to help prepare you for yours. If you are seeking a newborn and will need day care to return to work, speak with other new moms to get their recommendations.

- Let your employer know you are adopting and look into your options for taking maternity leave.

- A pediatrician is going to become a valuable resource for you as your child grows and develops. Interview different prospects and ask them important questions to ensure their philosophy is in line with yours.
- Find support groups for new moms in your area. If you live in a larger city or suburb, you may be fortunate enough to find adoption support groups. These can be a valuable network, especially if adopting internationally or an older child.
- Read, read, read! Prepare for parenthood by reading books on adoptive parenting and general parenting. Prepare for the age your child will be when you welcome them home and discuss issues like discipline and parenting style now with your spouse.
- Prepare to preserve and share your child's heritage with them, especially if it differs substantially from your own. If your child may have unique or different ethnic needs, plan now in order to minimize frustration down the road. For example, if you are adopting an African American child, you may need to learn about their specific hair care needs.
- It is common for adoptive parents to experience a letdown once the child is home. After months, or even years, of time-consuming preparation and anxiety, the sudden shift may seem anti-climactic. With infant or toddler adoptions, sleep deprivation can compound the problem. If you find yourself feeling down, consult a counselor or talk with other adoptive parents about how they coped.
- While there is no doubt about the heart-swelling love you feel for your new child, be sure to find a balance. Leave room in your life for your spouse, family, and friends, and take time for fun activities that provide a break from the responsibilities of new parenthood. A scheduled once-a-week diversion like date night is a sure remedy to burnout!
- Be realistic and patient. Your new family is real life, not a fairytale. Despite your best intentions and your best efforts, things are not likely to fall happily into place immediately, especially if you are adopting an older child. Allow everyone time to adjust. Most important, even if things are amazingly smooth in the beginning, prepare yourself mentally for the ups and downs that are sure to come with parenting any child.
- Create an emergency support network. Know whom you can call for everything from medical emergencies to last-minute babysitting. Be sure you can count on the people you select, and try to line up more than one for each contingency. For example, if you are delayed at work and can't pick your child up from day care, make sure there is someone besides your spouse who can fill in for you.

## Parenting and Beyond

It's a funny thing about parenting...the years slip by quickly, and even though you think you will remember every minute of your child's life, you unfortunately won't. As new milestones occur, you tend to forget or lose track of the earlier ones. To preserve every precious moment keep a diary, shoot videos, or take photos. Record things like baby's first words or your preschooler reciting a favorite poem or singing a song.

Decide how you will keep memorabilia of your child such as artwork, school papers, and awards, and file these things right away to avoid an overwhelming task down the road. Frame special mementos, such as the child's first drawing and first attempt at writing. Bronze the first pair of baby shoes. Turn the first baby blanket into a sentimental wall hanging. Childhood happens only once, record as much of it as you can. Above all, take time to enjoy these fleeting moments of parenthood. Relish in your success. You did it—you are now a family!

*"Be joyful always; pray continually; give thanks in all circumstances, for this is God's will for you in Christ Jesus."*
1 Thessalonians 5:16-18

## Answering Your Questions

*During the journey and wait of adoption, what is the single most important thing Christian families can do?*

When I was in the process of adoption, the power of prayer was undeniable. Each and every step of the way, I knew the Lord was walking with me. We often need a reminder, and I found that having a prayer bracelet around my wrist helped in my faith and hope of adoption we all need and want.

After I adopted, I designed an adoption prayer bracelet to encourage families in their adoption journey. They are daily reminders to pray for the child God has for us specifically and that we long for through adoption. My prayer is that by your act of faith, your dreams will come true, too.

*We know families who have waited a long time and others who seemed to have no wait at all. Can we do things that will affect our adoption wait time?*

Remember, much of your wait time will be determined by the path to adoption that you have chosen and your preferences in regards to a child. Your adoption professional should be able to give you an estimate so you have at least a general idea of what to expect.

While waiting to adopt, don't place your life on hold. Continue to plan, travel, take classes, volunteer, and bless others. This time of waiting is still a time of living. Sometimes this is the hardest tip to remember when it feels like your future is wrapped up in the wait. For me, I worked one hour each day on my adoption, then put it away, both physically (as in my files and paperwork) and emotionally.

Take time to learn more about the Biblical truths surrounding waiting on the Lord. This can be a powerful time for those who use it to do more than simply wait.

## ADOPTION WISDOM

God promises that He will fulfill your desire to be a parent. Although, when everyone around you already has a child or is getting pregnant, it can be a challenge to remember. Hold fast to His promises, like this one in Isaiah:

*"Do not be afraid, for I am with you;*
*I will bring your children from the east and gather you from the west."*
**Isaiah 43:5**

CHAPTER EIGHT

# WHEN THINGS GO WRONG

*"Through whom we have gained access by faith into this grace in which
we now stand. And we rejoice in the hope of the glory of God. Not only so,
but we also rejoice in our sufferings, because we know that suffering
produces perseverance; perseverance, character; and character, hope.
And hope does not disappoint us, because God has poured out His love into
our hearts by the Holy Spirit, whom He has given us."*
Romans 5:2-5

Challenges arise in adoption, just as they do in our everyday life and spiritual life. Make time to prepare for the difficult times in order to be better equipped should adoption challenges arise. This is the time when becoming educated about the adoption process and asking questions along the way will be an invaluable investment. Ensuring that seasoned adoption professionals are on your team will help in these times, as well. Put the energy into your plan that is required. Remember, your family is the most important thing you will ever build!

## Top Six Adoption Blunders

It is my hope that by sharing some of these embarrassing mistakes, you won't fall prey to them, and your adoption journey will be filled with peace and calm without guilt or regrets. Here are the six most common adoption blunders:

1. Not reading your adoption agreement or contract.
2. Making decisions from your heart and not your head and heart together.
3. Going against the recommendations of your adoption professional regarding a birth mother, such as giving her money.
4. Putting off completing the required paperwork.
5. Going back on your word regarding contact with the birth family after your adoption is final.

6. Not including God in your adoption plan, spending time in prayer, and listening to Him.

If you have already made these common adoption blunders, you can correct your direction and still find peace. Here are some simple solutions:

- If you have a contract you have not read, you can go back and read it now, if your adoption is not complete. Ask questions of your adoption professional. It is not too late!
- If you have already made decisions with your heart and have heartache to show for it, learn from it. Next time, take a deep breath and look at all sides of a situation before you jump in or commit. Also, forgive yourself.
- If you have paid a woman posing as a birth mother or one that was considering adoption and you just thought it would be okay to pay a few expenses behind your adoption professional's back, learn from this. In some states, expenses are illegal, and you don't want to do anything to jeopardize your adoption finalization. When in doubt, ask.
- I am constantly surprised at the number of adoptive parents who put off doing their home study and other paperwork and then miss adoption opportunities. They find out it is going to cost more to get it done when they needed it done "yesterday." If you have a home study that was completed more than 12 months ago, contact your home study provider to see when it expires and document this in your calendar. If it is expired, inquire on the home study update process and cost and then make a point of getting it done within 30 days. Only you can do this.
- If you have forgotten to stay in touch with your birth family, now is the time to consider: where you would be without her? I know I would not be a mommy without my children's birth families, and because of that, I want to always respect our agreements. Take time today to prepare a letter for your birth parents. A simple card with a photo or note letting them know you are thinking of them will be treasured. It does not take away from your role as parents, but will respect your child and how they came to be yours through their first family. You will be blessed for honoring your commitment.
- Finally, if you have left God out of your adoption plans, spend time in prayer right now to rededicate you adoption journey to Him. Seek prayer from your church family and counsel from your pastor if you are struggling with this step. God is always near and wants to be included in your journey to find the child that He has waiting for you.

# Re-Adopts

A few years ago, I assisted in an adoption of a bright, happy two-year-old boy who had been living with his grandmother. The adoptive parents that were chosen started the process of adoption but discovered four months later that they were pregnant. They called, asking if they could "return" him. I was sad and concerned at their lack of dedication to parenting, but my priority was this sweet child.

The grandmother was rightfully shocked and mistrusting of the whole adoption process. It was difficult for her to trust again and continue with adoption. Similarly, it made it hard for the child to bond with a new family and not be fearful that they, too, would leave.

To best prevent this situation, ensure that you, your spouse, and your family members are ready to parent with dedication, no matter what happens in the future. Is your personality one that is dedicated and loyal to the end? Answer this question honestly for the sake of a child. Learn and ask about the needs ahead of time so you know what to expect. Be honest in evaluating what you can and can't handle and seek God's guidance.

If a new adoptive family is needed, normally one can be found within a short period of time. Some circumstances might arise because of divorce or death of an adoptive parent, and then re-adopts can occur.

For example, currently in our center we are receiving re-adopt requests primarily from adoptive families who have adopted internationally, only to learn that the child has special needs they were not prepared for. Whenever older children are adopted, it is recommended that parents be prepared for and read books about attachment issues. They should also seek help before the situation is dire.

# Unexpected Challenges at Birth

We all know of situations where a pregnancy has progressed normally, prenatal care has been regular and routine, and then on the day of delivery, something doesn't go as planned. In adoption, this may be a medical condition, a positive drug test, or even a child of a different race than expected. For some families, the faith in the knowledge that God will provide propels them forward to completing the adoption as planned. Others may panic and flee the hospital. Be prepared and always seek guidance from your adoption professional before deciding one way or another.

This is one of the times walking with God will help you know what to do. Perhaps this is, indeed, the child He has for you, or perhaps you are simply an angel to this child for a short period of time, until the family God intends for her arrives. Either way, this is a time for patience, grace, and love.

Should you be confronted by a situation like this, the best option is to call your adoption professional or the 24-Hour Adoption Answer Line (1-800-923-6784) and ask the questions you need.

## WHEN IT'S NOT YOUR BABY

Birth mother Vanessa called us for the first time from the hospital. She was in labor, wanting to make an adoption plan and was happy to let us choose the adoptive family. She reported that she was having a Caucasian baby and denied any use of drugs or alcohol. Because time was of the essence, we called Jim and Suzanne, who lived only a few hours away from the hospital.

All was seemingly progressing well, until we got a call the next morning from a frantic Suzanne. Vanessa had fled the hospital after she found the hospital had tested her baby for drugs and the results had come back positive.

"We just can't do this! We can't have a drug baby," she said. "We weren't open to it, and it's not what we want." I listened and allowed her to share her concerns. I explained how she could help this baby by staying at the hospital until we could get another family there who was open to adopting a child with drug exposure.

"It's over," Suzanne said. "We're almost home now." My heart stopped. No birth mother, no adoptive mother, and a newborn that tested positive for drugs remained alone at the hospital.

We immediately contacted the hospital, but it was too late. Child Protective Services had been called, and this child would be lost to the foster care system. If things worked out for the best, Vanessa's rights were terminated quickly and this baby boy was available for adoption before he turned one. If things dragged on, he could now be a teen, having never known a stable home. Sadly, we'll never know.

If you feel unable to move forward, they can assist you in finding another family that is open to loving and parenting this child. **It is of the utmost importance that you not leave the child or announce to hospital staff that you are not moving forward.** Let your adoption professional handle that for you, in order for them to take the steps they need to find the family God has meant for this baby.

## Disagreements at Home

Katie and Steve were a lovely couple, who had made all the preparations to adopt their first child. They were quickly chosen by a woman who, like them, was in her mid-30's and had a career in real estate. It seemed to be a match truly made in heaven! The pregnancy progressed, and about four weeks before delivery, Katie called me in tears.

"Steve confessed to me last night that he had no desire for children. He says it is him or a baby," she said through her sobs. "I love my husband, but I know that God is leading this adoption. What do I do?"

We discussed the situation, and the couple made a quick visit with their pastor, which only seemed to confirm that Steve had no desire to share his life with a child.

I shared the news with the birth mother, and she shared Katie's resolve that this adoption was God's plan. She was open to proceeding with Katie as a single mom. The adoption was thankfully completed easily after the required legal changes were made to the home study and pre-adoption paperwork.

Katie is now a beautiful, Godly mother to daughter Kayla and has a very special relationship with Kayla's birth mother.

Some disagreements, like this, are resolved while keeping the adoption plan intact. Many more, however, are a loss for everyone. There is no way to plan or prepare for situations like this, but open communication is always the key. Even the strongest of relationships will be tested by parenthood. Be sure that you have the solid foundation you need before you begin building your family.

Now is the time for counseling if you find yourselves unequally yoked in any aspect of your life together.

## A Birth Mother Changes Her Mind

One of the biggest fears of adopting families is that a birth mother will change her mind at the last minute. And occasionally, it does happen.

Adoption is a matter of the heart. Even birth mothers with the best of reasons for choosing adoption often are overwhelmed with emotion and hormones after giving birth. This the hour for grace.

Without the precious sacrifice that birth mothers make, many of us would not be parents. Giving a birth mother time with her child, time to create a memory, time to say hello so that she can prepare to say goodbye will be a reassurance that you love and care for her, as well as her baby.

*"A new command I give you; Love one another.*
*As I have loved you, so you must love one another."*
John 13:34

When you hear those words, "I just can't do it," stay faithful. It is heartbreaking. You may feel as though God has forsaken you and your adoption journey, but He will pull you through. Ask for prayer, both for you and your birth mother. Rededicate your adoption to Him and have faith His plan will work for good.

Your birth mother is likely torn between emotion and reality. She may know she can't provide the life she wants for her baby, but she just can't say goodbye. She knows she is hurting you, but her heart is breaking, too.

Perhaps her situation has changed, her family has offered help at the last minute, or the father of her baby has re-entered her life, and she feels able to parent. Regardless of her situation, let her know that you aren't upset and will still be happy to adopt her child should she decide that adoption is best.

This happened in my son's adoption. His birth mother reclaimed after delivering, only to call me five weeks after our son's birth.

"I've tried," she said weakly. "I just can't do it. Would you still consider adopting him?" It was a bittersweet moment. While I knew this was God's plan to make me a mother, I also knew it required a sacrifice from her.

If you experience a reclaim, understand that this is a time to lean heavily on each other, on Him, and on your adoption professional. Let your adoption professional follow-up with the birth mother and be an intermediary as the match dissolves. Allow yourselves to grieve together the loss of this adoption. It is a very real loss, and it will require time to heal.

My best advice to you is to reserve a little piece of your heart from any adoption until you know that the consents to adoption are irrevocable. You want to be sure that you are cautiously optimistic and faithfully walking with Him through <u>any</u> match.

> *"'For I know the plans I have for you,' declares the Lord,*
> *'plans to prosper you and not to harm you,*
> *plans to give you hope and a future.'"*
> Jeremiah 29:11

**PERSEVERANCE**
I know it is hard to have a reclaim happen. I have been there. Thankfully, it doesn't happen to everyone, but when it happens to you, it is "everyone." I do believe the Lord doesn't give us more than we can handle and that birth mothers who change their mind are part of His plan, too. I can't imagine not having our son, and I wouldn't have him if it weren't for the reclaim before him.

## Coming Home Without a Child

Increasingly, I am hearing stories of families traveling for international adoption, only to return home childless. This breaks my heart. Often, this occurs when they meet the child and learn that he or she has more needs than the family was previously informed.

For example, I recently met a couple who traveled to Eastern Europe to adopt a healthy three-year-old girl, only to discover that she had cerebral palsy. The self-employed couple with emergency-only type health insurance was not prepared to parent a child with lifelong medical special needs.

Both international and domestic adoptions carry a small risk of a couple returning home without a child. For this reason, I encourage families to wait on having baby showers or similar celebrations until after things are more certain. It may also be beneficial to keep your adoption match and travel on somewhat of a "need to know" basis. Close friends and family members will want to help and comfort you, but you may not wish to have to explain things over and over again to casual acquaintances.

Be patient with each other during this time. Your expectations have been shattered, and your adoption may feel far away. Have faith in His plan and take the time you need to grieve your loss before moving forward with another adoption.

*"Trust in the Lord with all your heart and lean not on your own understanding; in all your ways acknowledge Him, and He will make your paths straight."*
Proverbs 3:5,6

## Adoption Fraud and Scams

Adoption fraud occurs when someone posing as a birth mother or an adoption professional works to convince you that, with the payment of a fee or certain expenses, you can adopt a specific child. The best way to avoid adoption fraud is through the use of an experienced and reliable adoption professional.

Some of the most common scams in adoption are also some of the most heart-breaking stories or appealing situations, including:

* **Orphans from the African nation of Cameroon.** These stories are frequently seen by families who are looking for an adoption situation on their own, without a professional. Contact usually is through email. Unfortunately, many families have fallen prey to the request for funds to help with travel in order to move an adoption along. If you see anything referring to Cameroon, do not pursue it, no matter how sad the story may seem. If you do wish to investigate a bit further, pass the information on to your adoption professional so they may dig a little deeper into the possibilities.
* **Adoption situations offering twins or triplets,** especially when the birth mother states that she does not wish to speak with your adoption attorney or

### He is there when we need Him.

Sometimes, it feels as if God has forgotten us, but be assured if you have a relationship with our Heavenly Father. He is there with you and is the never changing, amazing God that knows our needs before we know them. He knows your heart and desires for being a parent.

When you need Him, He is there. Trust Him to love you where you are and to meet your needs in His timing. He will take your hand and guide you along the road through the bumps and rocky paths, as well as the soft and gentle ways.

licensed adoption facilitator. Even when you have what seems like a solid proof of pregnancy, do be diligent and confirm it. This is a frequent and attractive situation for fraud. Adoptive parents think it is beneficial to adopt two or more children at a time, and at times it can be. Some adoptive parents have gone against their better judgment, taking risks just in case it is not a scam. Proceed with caution whenever a multiple birth is offered.

- **Asking for money right away with a desperate story.** This is an increasingly common scam, with people posing as birth parents demanding money immediately, threatening to call another family if you don't comply. I have even worked with women who said if they didn't receive cash now, they would abort their babies, and it would be my fault. Remember never provide money unless it is with the permission of your attorney and adoption professional. And, when possible, pay the expenses directly to the vendor, such as the electric company or landlord.

- **Adoption situations "shopped" around.** If it seems too good to be true, it probably is. If an adoption "professional" has to actively advertise to find a family for an appealing adoption situation, there is likely cause for raised eyebrows. Most adoption professionals never have to look outside of their own pool of waiting families to find a match, unless the birth mother requests are extremely specific or the child has special medical needs. These are situations that cause "stacked" fees, meaning each party that handles the request adds another fee to the situation for themselves. The result is a number of "intermediaries" receiving money for simply passing an adoption situation along. Proceed with *extreme* caution, as most monies paid for any situation like this will be lost if the adoption falls through, or will lock you in with an adoption "professional" whom you did not choose.

- **Adoption "professionals" that request a fee to show you to one particular situation**. This is a common way of locking you into a long-term agreement because you have already given them the first $1,000 or so for a birth mother that didn't choose you. Now, you are more likely to stay there since you've already "invested" with them. Pass on this type of arrangement.

> Trust, but verify, each situation you consider.
> Because adoption is a matter of the heart,
> this advice cannot be underestimated.

## Answering Your Questions

*After going through an adoption scam, how can we trust someone again?*

It isn't easy, that's for sure! My advice to any family who has been through this type of situation is to learn from it and see where you could have seen red flags previously. Even if there weren't any red flags, leave that situation in the past. You cannot carry baggage or hurt feelings from that situation, or it may sabotage the next opportunity to adopt.

Pray that your heart can forgive the person or people who took advantage of you and move on. God has blessings in store for you, but your hands must be open to accept them, not clenching the heartbreak from the past.

*Nothing went wrong with our adoption, but now I just feel sad and blue. Is this normal?*

Yes, Post-Adoption Depression Syndrome (PADS) is a very real experience. Just like new mothers experience Post-Partum Depression, PADS is thought to be a result of sudden changes that may include 24-hour care of another person, increased financial drains, lack of personal time, and any other of the sudden changes that involve bringing a child into your family. It may also be part of a normal "let-down" after attaining any major milestone in life.

Seek professional help and counseling. It does not mean that there is anything wrong with you, but you may just need a little help getting through this period of adjustment and new responsibilities. Men may be affected, as well, so be sure you are having active and ongoing communication about your feelings, seeking counseling together, if needed. And don't neglect your walk with God.

# ADOPTION WISDOM

As children of the Father, we know to call on Him when we need strength, guidance, and peace. Yet there are times that the answers are not always clear, the possibilities are not laid before us in neat order, and our prayers may seem like they aren't getting past the ceiling.

Spend time in the Word, learn your options, pray for those helping you, as well as those who may challenge your goals, and remember that though some days may feel dark, He will never desert you.

*"Never will I leave you, Never will I forsake you."*
**Hebrews 13:5**

CHAPTER NINE

# A SPECIAL NOTE ON
# RESOLVING INFERTILITY

*Sometimes, in the midst of trying to conceive, taking pregnancy tests, and experiencing
monthly failures, it can seem difficult to see past the unfulfilled dream of parenthood.
Yet through it all, God sees you for the treasure you are.*

*He sees the value you offer to the world, when you may not feel you have much to offer.
He sees your worth, when you may not feel worthy of Him.
Much like a diamond has no concept of the value it holds or the beauty it is,
you, too, may not be able to see your own value and beauty.*

**"God created man in His own image."**
Genesis 1:27

Did you know that right now, over 2 million married women are
experiencing infertility? 11.8% of all American women are unable to conceive a
child after trying for one year. Some will go on to have a biological child; others
will not. And each year, over 60,000 couples from all walks of life will adopt
because they share a belief that their lives will not be complete without a child.

Since fertility declines with age and so many women are pursuing careers,
trouble conceiving is common among those who wait to start families. The most
proven method is in vitro fertilization (IVF) where eggs are drawn from the
ovaries and fertilized in a lab dish with concentrated sperm. Grown for three
days into tiny embryos, several are placed in the uterus. If attempted for five
cycles, this will make a baby in one out of three patients. The cost? About $15,000
per cycle.

Driven by a seemingly desperate need, some couples have spent over
$150,000 on this procedure. Along with the financial toll, comes an emotional
one, as well. Repeated failure is felt mostly by the woman, and many marriages
cannot thrive during this time. Sadly, when families have invested so heavily

into failed fertility attempts, they may have no financial resources left for adoption.

Even when IVF does succeed, many are challenged by the dilemma of "left-over" embryos or reducing a pregnancy when doctors recommend this as a measure of increasing the chance of carrying just one baby to term. As Christians, many would never consider some of these options, but the moral dilemmas remain, often resulting in unthinkably difficult choices to make.

I believe that the desire to be a parent is from Him, yet how we approach that desire when biological pregnancy does not happen easily also needs to include His plans for us. While many of us are called to become parents, few of us are called to adoption.

## Coming to Terms with My Infertility

As the oldest of five children, I had one sister and three brothers. I loved and helped care for them from the time when I was quite young. Mothering came naturally to me, and by the age of 11, I knew when I grew up, more than anything else, I wanted to be a mother.

I collected clothes and quilted a baby blanket that I kept in a hope chest for the child I would have one day. I fell in love with a man who also wanted children. He especially wanted to have a son he could teach to fish, ride a bicycle, and play baseball. From the first days after our wedding, we set out to have a family.

The months went by, then two years passed, but no baby came. Couples all around us seemed to get pregnant without even trying. I must have gone to a dozen baby showers during those early years of our marriage. I laughed with my friends as the expectant mothers opened their gifts, but I was crying inside.

We decided to see specialists, and we discovered that we both had fertility problems. Starting in the spring of 1985, I remember the months starting as a blur of tests and fertility drugs, another ovulation on the temperature chart, more poking and prodding, the start of one more menstrual cycle.

I came to dread holiday gatherings because of the humiliating questions. Getting dressed before one New Year's Eve party, we took bets on how many insults we'd hear that night. He said 10, and that was about right. The topper was when my Grandpa asked at the dinner table, "Haven't you figured out how to *do* it yet?"

"We lost that page of the manual," I said with a smile, though his words had pierced me to the bone.

Some friends I had confided in offered remedies they said had worked for people they knew. We were supposed to eat fish twice a day, make love on the night of a full moon, and I was to lie on a propped up board that stood me on my head. I started to avoid those friends and even my business associates, fearing that someone would ask when we were going to have children or if I was pregnant yet. We continued to see a specialist who was growing less hopeful.

As the months passed, life did not seem so bright. As the owner of a medium-sized manufacturing company, I had come to believe that if you wanted something bad enough, worked hard and smart enough, you could have it. But that didn't seem to help with pregnancy. As the CEO, I came to expect that when I needed something, I could pick up the phone and have it delivered. But I could not order a baby.

In my spiritual life, I came to wonder, since I was sure that God wanted us to have children, why He had not blessed us with a family. Was I doing something wrong? I prayed for an answer and prayed for a baby.

An avid reader, I bought books on infertility and human reproduction, on infant care and early childhood development. I hoped that somehow a baby might pop up out of a book as a result of all my studies! I went to the library almost every day (there was no Internet yet), and the librarian became my friend. One morning, she gave me a book on adoption. I took it over to a table and set it down. I sat in the chair and looked at its cover, but I could not bring myself to open it. I pushed it away and got on with my research into getting pregnant.

When I left the library, I set the adoption book next to me in the passenger seat of my car and took it home. Finally that night, I opened it and started to read. It was scary, because it was about 15 years out of date and written about the old ways of adopting, which seemed cold, secretive, and formal. Then I read another book about modern adoption, which seemed warm, honest, and comfortable.

After some really bad news from our doctor, my husband and I lay in bed one night talking. I saw that the door to adoption was opening, just as the door to getting pregnant seemed to be closing shut.

Within days, we decided to adopt. Right away, it seemed like there was light shining into our lives again. We were excited about our future with children. Adoption was the answer to my questions and to my prayers.

## Resolving Fertility Issues

Sometimes I see people rush into adoption without taking the time to grieve the loss of the biological child they did not have. They risk sabotaging an adoption or, worse, treating the child they adopt as second best to the son or daughter they might have had biologically.

Before you can adopt with success, you must come to terms with your infertility. Pray and seek confirmation – this takes time. Move at your own pace, but realize that you are not getting any younger, and the longer you wait, the more you delay the precious time you could have with the child God has meant for your family.

For me, coming to terms with infertility meant accepting that there was a reason for everything. I don't know why I was unable to have babies, but were it not for my infertility, I would not have adopted my wonderful son. I would not have opened an adoption center that has brought thousands of children and parents together, changing their lives.

I have known many couples who have faced infertility and moved on quite naturally to adoption. I have known others who have edged toward it uneasily, because their dream of having a biological child meant so much to them. Before you are ready to adopt, you have to know the answer to this question: Do you want to be a parent, or do you want to have a biological child?

You may feel as though you must *settle* for adoption. You cannot do this. A child deserves to have parents who love and cherish him as the most precious gift on earth. If you have unresolved issues about infertility, seek prayer and counseling before you adopt. You may choose to put adoption aside and press on with medical treatment until you have exhausted all options. Then, when you return to take up adoption, you may find, as many people do, that the adoption process is less stressful and more enjoyable than your infertility treatments. If you are not sure you can accept a child who will not inherit your genes, it may help you to talk with other adoptive parents or a counselor.

We are still amazed by the traits and characteristics that parents pass on to their adopted children. Like the adopted daughter whose sweet southern accent sounds just like her mother, or the son who has the same walk as his adoptive father, the same crinkling of his eyes when he laughs. Even biblically, Joseph, as Jesus' adoptive father, passed on the skills and talents of carpentry.

As with many things in life, we can only see God's beautiful plan as we look back to see how He was working to bless and care for us along our journey.

---

*Dear Lifetime Staff,*

*Well...it's been a whole year, and we are still in disbelief!! We still marvel at our daughter and how much joy she has brought us, as well as our entire family. Looking back through all of our trials with infertility, we just could not see or understand what God's plan was for us. Now, looking at our daughter, we understand. All the sorrow and tears that we had for so many years seemed to disappear instantly with her birth. We are so looking forward to our lives as a family—Life could not be happier!*

*Always,*
*Dave & Tiffany.*

---

## Answering Your Questions

*How do you know when it's time to move on from fertility treatments?*

I wish there was a simple answer. For me, it was when I realized that I wanted to be a mother more than I wanted to have a biological child. Adoption could make that happen for me.

You see, choosing adoption doesn't have to mean giving up on being pregnant. I just knew that I was ready to be a mommy and God was leading me toward the dream down a different road. A number of years later, I was blessed with a successful pregnancy, but I never questioned the unique way my family came together.

Spend time together talking and praying about what each of you wants for your family. Adoption doesn't have to be closing the door on pregnancy, just be sure you know how your adoption professional feels about a pregnancy while adopting. At our center, we will place your file on hold during this time and start up again when so advised. Other organizations may have different policies, so be sure you ask.

---

### A MESSAGE TO YOU FROM MARDIE

Infertility sometimes feels as though your body doesn't work correctly.

Perhaps it is just God calling you to another purpose, another part of His perfect plan? He is calling you to be more than you are and to love a child born outside of your womb, yet inside of your heart.

*"Do you not know that your body is a temple of the Holy Spirit, who is in you, whom you have received from God? You are not your own; you were bought at a price."*
**1 Corinthians 6:19,20**

---

CHAPTER TEN

# A FEW FINAL NOTES

After helping thousands of adoptive parents find their way through the journey of adoption, I can say unequivocally that God's hand is at work today. I have a beautiful perspective from which to see Him guiding these precious children to the home that He ultimately desires for them.

I believe that He also has a plan for you and for your child. Trust in His guidance and His plans for you. And never forget that there is a baby for you!

I want to share a few final notes with you about keeping God a part of your adoption journey. This was the key to my adoption success, and I pray it will be the central focus of yours, as well.

## On Fellowship...

*"They devoted themselves to the apostles' teaching and to the fellowship, to the breaking of bread and to prayer. Everyone was filled with awe, and many wonders and miraculous signs were done by the apostles. All the believers were together and had everything in common."*
Acts 2:42-44

It is important to have Christian fellowship throughout the course of your adoption—before, during, and after. Surround yourselves with those who understand what you are going through. They need to lift you up and not beat you down when they don't understand what you are feeling during your wait for a baby or as your adoption becomes final. Many people don't have enough experience in adoption as it is today and, therefore, can't be as helpful as someone who has been in your shoes and has had the same fears and concerns as only adoptive parents have.

## On Prayer...

*"For where two or three come together in my name,*
*there am I with them."*
Matthew 18:20

Pray together, as a couple, for the Lord to bless your adoption journey. Pray for patience and wisdom, and use this time together with the Lord to grow your relationship spiritually as you wait to grow your family. Encourage each other, and pray for each other. Adoption is not always an easy road, but with faith, you will be blessed.

It is imperative to be around people who have the same heart and can pray for you and your adoption needs. This can be an online group or a prayer partner.

## On Faith...

*"Do not let your heart be troubled.*
*Trust in God; trust also in me."*
John 14:1

The Lord wants you to succeed and not fail. You need to know that the Lord has a plan for your life and for your family—this must be ingrained in your mind and your heart. Pray for faith and guidance as you seek the blessing of a family. Implement the faith God provides by preparing your home for your new baby. Maintaining your faith is easier when you truly believe by acting on it.

## On Frustration...

*"In all your ways acknowledge Him*
*and He will make your paths straight."*
Proverbs 3:6

Remember, authentic faith allows for true emotion with a sincere trust that God is there in and through it. Step out in faith and listen to what God wants for your life. When you are frustrated, bring it to the Lord and pray about it. Thousands of women and men have been in the same place you are in today and have felt the same—*Will we ever be parents? Why am I not a parent? What have I done wrong?* Do not focus on the negative, but look up at what God wants for you specifically.

*"The Lord is my strength and my shield;*
*my heart trusts in Him, and I am helped.*
*My heart leaps for joy,*
*and I will give thanks to Him in song."*
Psalm 28:7

## On the Future...

*"As for me and my household, we will serve the Lord."*
Joshua 24:15

Remember, families created through adoption are true families, as illustrated throughout the Bible and still today. After adoption, you are a parent, and your child will depend on you for his physical, spiritual, and emotional needs. All the joys and heartaches any parent experiences will be yours. You will be Mom and Dad.

May God richly bless you as you answer His call to adoption!

## AN ADOPTION PRAYER

*"I know that You can do all things; no plan of Yours can be thwarted."*
Job 42:2

Heavenly Father,
Your good and gracious nature is to give me my heart's desire. I long to raise a child. Is adoption Your will for my life? If You are calling me to adopt, please make my path clear and provide me with the tools, perseverance, and eager heart to take steps toward my future child.

I give thanks for the trials that have led me to discern Your call to adoption and ask that You continue to walk with me, pulling me closer to You as I begin a new journey. I trust Your lead and place my hope in You. Help me answer You willingly, if You are indeed calling me to adopt.

In Christ's name, I give glory to You for all You have given me,
and for Your blessings yet to come!
Amen

# ADOPTION GLOSSARY

For your convenience, the following glossary includes terms that are commonly used by social workers, attorneys, licensed facilitators, agencies, and other adoption professionals. Each may have a slightly different nuance in international adoption and may vary somewhat from state to state.

**Abandonment:** Desertion of a child by a birth parent or guardian with no provisions for continued childcare or evidence of intent to return. When the birth parent has not had contact for an amount of time specified in state law, a father/mother has abandoned a child. See *Legalized Abandonment*.

**Adoptee:** A child who is adopted and joins a family through adoption.

**Adoption Assistance Program/Adoption Assistance Payment (AAP):** Adoption subsidies authorized and funded by federal law, Title 42, Chapter 7, Subchapter IV, Part E. Administered by individual states to assist prospective parents who are adopting and caring for children with special needs. Children not covered under Title IV-E may be eligible for state subsidies. Contact your local social service agency.

**Adoption:** A social and legal process that establishes the relationship of parent and child between people who do not have this relationship by birth. It provides the same rights and obligations that exist between children and their biological parents.

**Adoption Agency:** A public, private for-profit, or private not-for-profit agency licensed by a state to provide services to birth parents, adoptive parents, and adoptive children. Agencies may perform home studies and can do all or some of the required legal and social work. Some agencies offer full-service adoptions, including preparation of the home study, coordination of birth family intakes, and placement of the child in the adoptive family's home. Some agencies provide home studies for independent adoptions, allowing families to find birth mothers with the help of an attorney or an adoption facilitator.

**Adoption Assistance:** Any financial help given to adoptive parents. See *AAP*.

**Adoption Attorney:** A legal professional who specializes in adoption law and is experienced with filing, processing, and finalizing adoptions in court. Some attorneys provide assistance with locating a child, speaking to birth parents, requesting medical records, networking with attorneys in the birth mother's state, and providing all requisite adoption services, with the exception of the home study. Others prefer to process only the adoption paperwork. Some attorneys work with adoption facilitators to locate birth mothers for their clients, while others prefer prospective parents to find birth mothers on their own through other resources.

**Adoption Benefits:** Employee-sponsored benefits, often comparable to maternity leave, that are provided to adoptive parents. Benefits may include monetary reimbursement for the expenses of adopting a child, financial assistance, or parental or family leave in connection with the adoption.

**Adoption Consultant**: An adoption advisor who does not work directly with birth parents. Advisors often offer profile assistance and provide situations from attorneys and agencies for consideration. They work as a "middle man" between adoptive families and an adoption professional. Most families do not need an adoption consultant when using qualified and experienced adoption professionals. Consultants are not licensed adoption facilitators.

**Adoption Decree:** A document signed by a judge and issued by the court upon finalization of an adoption. The decree states that the adoptee is the legal child of the adoptive parents, who are granted legal custody.

**Adoption Disruption**: The interruption of an adoption plan prior to finalization that results in the child leaving the adoptive home. This may occur because the adoptive parents change their minds (also known as a failed adoption), because the birth parents revoke consent (also known as a reclaim), or because it is deemed that the adoptive parents are endangering the child or are not complying with requirements set by the agency (also known as a failed placement).

**Adoption Dissolution**: The interruption or "failure" of an adoption after finalization. This requires court action and can be initiated by the adoptive parents or the courts, but not by the birth parents.

**Adoption Exchange:** A program that helps facilitate adoption placements. Organizations involved in adoption exchange help generate matches by sharing information about available children and prospective parents. Exchanges may provide advocacy, training, support, and resource services, as well as referrals for adoption agencies and adoptive families. Exchanges are typically run by state departments of human services and some work across state lines.

**Adoption Facilitator:** A professional organization or individual who helps bring together birth families and prospective adoptive parents for the purpose of arranging an adoption plan for a child. They should be bonded and licensed where state laws permit, such as California. Facilitators usually locate and work directly with birth parents seeking to place a child for adoption. When working with prospective adoptive parents, some help only to find a child, while others follow an adoption to finalization. They do not handle the legal aspects of adoption or home studies. Some facilitators offer counseling by outside licensed sources. Laws vary from state to state regarding the payment and use of facilitators by a prospective adoptive family. In many cases, a qualified and experienced facilitator can prove to be a valuable asset and, as an adoption professional, can guide and assist families in the completion of an adoption.

**Adoption Home Study Report**: A comprehensive study and written report about the prospective adoptive family, including details such as family background and upbringing, lifestyle, medical history, financial statements, values, beliefs, interests, family support systems, and parenting styles. During the home study—which is conducted by a licensed social worker or other professional as designated by state law—the family is educated about the process of adoption, investigated for child abuse or criminal background, and taken through an in-depth series of interviews. Besides incorporating a background check on all adults living in the home, the study may include an FBI and/or state fingerprint check, if it is required by the state in which the birth mother lives. The home study includes several on-site visits and must be completed before a child is placed in the home.

**Adoption Insurance/Adoption Cancellation Insurance:** A policy that protects prospective adoptive parents against financial loss incurred when an adoption proceeding is underway and the birth parents decide not to place their child for adoption. This insurance is not always available and can be costly.

**Adoption Laws**: State regulations based on statutes and case law and enacted by the legislators who regulate adoptions. Birth parents, adoptive parents, and adoption professionals are required to comply with such laws. The state in which the birth mother resides or gives birth may have different laws than the state of residence for the adoptive family. An adoption attorney should be consulted when legal questions arise.

**Adoption Lawyer:** See *Adoption Attorney*.

**Adoption Petition:** A legal document in which prospective adoptive parents appeal to the state court for permission to adopt a specific child.

**Adoption Placement:** A process that begins when a child first lives with his or her prospective adoptive parents and continues until the adoption is finalized.

**Adoption Plan:** A distinct and individual plan made by biological parents for the adoption of their child. In addition to stating the decision to place the child for adoption, the plan may include specifics on the type of family the parents want to adopt their child, who will be present at the birth, and how much future contact they wish to have with the child and the adoptive parents.

**Adoption Profile**: Information on prospective adoptive parents presented to birth parents. This profile is used in many domestic adoptions. Also known as an Adoptive Parent Profile, Dear Birth Mother Letter, Résumé.

**Adoption Registry:** A reunion registry that allows adoptees, birth parents, and biological siblings to locate each other through a list of adoptees and birth relatives who have voluntarily offered their identifying information.

**Adoption Reversal:** The reclaiming of a child who has been voluntarily placed with adoptive parents by birth parents who have had a subsequent change of heart. Each state has enacted laws that define the time limits and circumstances under which a child may be reclaimed.

**Adoption Service Provider (ASP):** A licensed social worker who is certified by the state to assist birth parents and adoptive parents with the placement of a child in an Independent Adoption Placement.

**Adoption Subsidy:** See *AAP*.

**Adoption Tax Credits:** Non-refundable credits that may reduce taxes owed by adoptive parents who claim reimbursement for adoption expenses—such such as adoption fees, court fees, attorney fees, and travel expenses. This credit can be claimed on federal tax returns and, in some states, on state tax returns.

**Adoption Tax Exclusions:** Provisions in the federal tax code that allow adoptive parents to exclude any cash or adoption benefits for qualifying adoption expenses received from a private-sector employer when computing the family's adjusted gross income for tax purposes.

**Adoption Tax Identification Number (ATIN):** A temporary number used for a taxpayer's child if the child's adoption is pending. If an authorized adoption agency places a child in your home, you may be able to claim the child as your dependent and also claim the child- and dependent-care credit.

**Adoption Triad:** The three parties involved in an adoption: birth parents, adoptive parents, and adopted child/children. Also referred to as an adoption triangle or adoption circle.

**Adoptive Parent:** A person granted all the legal rights and responsibilities of a birth parent through a court-approved adoption.

**Adult Adoption:** The adoption of a person over the age of majority as defined by state law. In most states, an adult can legally adopt another adult as long as the adopting adult is at least 10 years older than the person being adopted.

**Affidavit:** A written legal document in which the signer swears under oath before a notary public or an authorized official that the statements in the document are true and correct to the best of his or her knowledge.

**Agency Adoption:** An adoption facilitated by either a public or private agency licensed by the state. While agency programs and services vary, most provide home study services to prospective adoptive parents, counseling to birth parents, birth parent relinquishment services, and post-placement follow-up. A social worker screens prospective adoptive parents and supervises the placement of children in adoptive homes until the adoption is finalized. Some agencies are full-service, offering features such as special-needs adoptions and both domestic and international adoption programs.

**Agency-Assisted Adoption:** An adoption facilitated by an agency that helps prospective parents complete the adoption once a child has been identified. Agencies handle the paperwork and finalization of the adoption and may provide services to both birth mothers and adoptive parents.

**Alleged Birth Father:** The alleged father of a child born out of wedlock, also referred to as a putative father or reputed father. A man is deemed to be the alleged, putative, or reputed father of a child if the birth mother claims that he is the father.

**Amended Birth Certificate:** A document issued after a child's adoption naming the adoptive parents as mother and father of the child. This certificate also states the name the adoptive parents have chosen for the child. Some states allow adoptees to obtain an uncertified copy of their original birth records prior to adoption by submitting a notarized written request. State laws vary and are changing yearly.

**Apostille:** A certificate—used in international adoptions and issued by the Secretary of State or equivalent—that verifies the legality and authenticity of documents such as birth certificates, marriage records, and home studies. The apostille provides expedited processing of documents for countries that are parties to the Hague Convention.

**Attachment:** An emotional connection founded in trust and forged with another individual. The inability to bond to a primary caregiver in the first 18 to 24 months of life may lead to reactive attachment disorder, a serious problem often found in abused or neglected children.

**Attachment Disorder/Reactive Attachment Disorder:** The inability to trust or love due to a break in the bonding cycle during infancy.

**Authentication:** In international adoptions, a procedure in which notarized and certified documents are viewed and approved by the consulate or embassy of the country from which the family is adopting.

**Birth Certificate (original):** A certified document indicating an individual's birth information, including mother's and father's names and the name given to the child at the time of birth. See *Amended Birth Certificate*.

**Birth Parent:** A child's biological or genetic parent. In the adoption arena, this term refers to parents who conceived and gave birth to a child, made an adoption plan for the child, and subsequently relinquished the child for adoption.

**Black Market Adoption:** The sale of infants by unscrupulous people for profit; an adoption in which one or more parties make a profit from a child placement, as opposed to an adoption in which certified professionals receive payment for providing counseling, child locating, and outreach.

**Bonding:** The formation of close specialized human relationships; the process of developing lasting emotional ties with one's primary caregiver(s); the first and fundamental developmental task of a human being which is central to the ability to form healthy relationships throughout a lifetime.

**Bonding Cycle:** The cycle of need. The expression of need (e.g. crying), gratification, and trust that is repeated time and time again between an infant and a primary caregiver throughout infancy.

**Certificate of Citizenship:** A document declaring the citizenship of an individual. Adoptive parents of children adopted internationally can obtain a U.S. Certificate of Citizenship by filing form N-643. This can be done immediately after the child arrives in the U.S. or after finalization of the adoption, depending on the child's type of visa (see *IR-3 vs. IR-4*). Once the child is granted citizenship, the full rights and privileges of United States citizenship are conferred. A Certificate of Citizenship differs from citizenship through naturalization, since the latter does not include full rights and privileges.

**Certification:** The judicial determination that a prospective adoptive parent is a fit and proper person to adopt. To receive certification for adoption, whether for a specific or unknown child, an individual must complete and submit a formal application for adoption, as well as a certification investigation and report. The components include:

- A completed Family and Home Application, including a financial statement
- Licensing/employment information for each adult member of the household
- A physician's report
- FBI fingerprint clearance

The application is reviewed and a recommendation made to the court regarding the suitability of the applicant to become an adoptive parent.

**Certified Document:** A copy of a document—such as a marriage license or birth certificate—obtained from, and validated by, a county or state. In international adoptions, certification for dossier purposes refers to documents that are notarized by a registered notary public, then forwarded to the Secretary of State's office for verification of the notary's signature. Documents can also be certified at a county level, a process sometimes referred to as a "juret." The type of certification required in international adoptions can vary by country. Families should check the dossier packet or speak with an attorney or adoption professional before certifying any documents.

**Child Abuse Clearances:** A method of determining whether an individual has a history of child abuse. This is part of the home study approval process for prospective adoptive and foster parents. Such clearances must be updated annually.

**Closed Adoption:** An adoption in which the birth parents and adoptive parents do not share any identifying information. A closed adoption supports total confidentiality and sealed records, with no contact or ongoing relationship among the parties involved.

**Concurrent Planning:** The process of planning to reunify a child with his or her birth family, while simultaneously investigating alternative placements with relatives or an adoptive family. Employing this process can reduce the time a child spends in temporary placements or foster care.

**Confidential Intermediary:** A government employee or trained individual sanctioned by the courts and allowed access to sealed adoption records for the purpose of finding information at the request of a member of an adoption triad. Any information obtained during the course of the investigation is kept strictly confidential, and is used to arrange contact between the individual who initiated the search and the sought-after biological relative, or for the purpose of obtaining consent for the release of adoption records. When an intermediary on behalf of another individual locates a biological relative, the intermediary must obtain consent from both parties, indicating that they wish to communicate with one another. Contact is made only when the court receives this consent. If consent for personal communication is not obtained from both parties, all relinquishment and adoption records and any information obtained by the confidential intermediary during the course of his or her investigation are returned to the court and remain confidential.

**Confidentiality:** A principle by which identifying or other significant data about a person is legally kept secret; nondisclosure of personal information without the consent of the individual involved.

**Consent:** The agreement by a parent—or a person or agency acting in place of a parent—to relinquish a child for adoption and release all rights and duties with respect to that child. Birth parents can legally change their minds about consent at any point before the birth of the child and up to the time their rights are terminated. State laws differ regarding the time frames when this consent may be given and withdrawn.

**Contact Veto:** A document filed by one party to an adoption that formally registers a refusal to be contacted by a searching party.

**Cooperative Adoption/Open Adoption:** A form of adoption in which some contact and exchange of information takes place among the birth family, the adoptive family, and the adoptee. Several options are possible and are determined by the parties involved.

**Co-parenting:** A seldom used, long-term, formal or informal agreement made between birth parents and adoptive parents to support the needs of adoptees.

**Counseling:** The provision of assistance and guidance by a trained professional to help resolve personal issues and difficulties, enabling an individual to assess situations, consider alternatives, and make decisions. Adoption counseling should be handled by experienced adoption counselors. Birth parent counseling may include the exploration of options, such as keeping and parenting the child; making an adoption plan that includes relatives, friends, or prospective adoptive parents; foster care; and various other types of temporary or permanent placements.

**Criminal Clearance:** A clearance through the State Police Department to determine if a person has a criminal record. Each state can supply the appropriate forms. In many states, the clearances must be updated on an annual basis. In adoptions, all adults living in a household must obtain criminal and child abuse clearances prior to the placement of a child in that home.

**Custody:** Protective care or guardianship. Foster parents do not have legal custody of the children placed in their care.

**De Facto:** A Latin term that essentially translates to "actually existing but not officially approved."

**De facto Adoption:** A legal agreement to adopt a child according to the laws of a particular state, eventually resulting in a legal adoption process once the adoption petition is filed with the appropriate court.

**Decree of Adoption:** A legal order that finalizes an adoption.

**Department of Human Services (DHS):** The state agency that handles adoptions and foster care for children in custody of the state, and employs the social service workers who conduct home studies. The name of the department varies by state, and can be called Department of Health and Social Services (DHSS) or Department of Social Services (DSS).

**Dependent Child:** A child who is temporarily or permanently in the custody of the county or state child welfare system.

**Designated Agency Adoption/Identified Adoptions:** A process by which birth parents choose their child's adoptive parents and authorize the placement of the child with the assistance of an adoption agency.

**Disclosure:** The release or transmittal of previously unknown information.

**Disclosure Veto:** A document filed by an individual disallowing the release of any identifying information about that person to another individual.

**Dossier:** A collection of papers containing detailed information about a particular person or subject; a set of legal documents used in an international adoption to process a child's adoption or assignment of guardianship in the foreign court.

**Domestic Adoption:** The adoption of a child living in the United States by a family in the United States.

**Disruption:** A situation in which a child leaves an adoptive home prior to the finalization of the adoption. Disruption can occur when the birth parents revoke their consent to the adoption, the adoptive parents decide not to proceed with the adoption, or the agency or court agent feels it is not in the best interest of the child to complete the adoption. The latter may be due to the family's noncompliance with requirements of the court or the belief that the child is endangered in some way.

**Dissolution:** An adoption that fails after finalization, resulting in the return of the adoptee to foster care or to another adoptive family. Birth parents may not dissolve an adoption, but adoptive parents may petition a court to do so. A judge may choose to allow or deny dissolution based on the likelihood that the family can remain intact and whether or not the child's ongoing presence is considered a threat to the child or the family.

**Equitable Adoption:** A legal process that establishes the inheritance rights of a child when a prospective adoptive parent clearly indicates the wish to adopt the child, placement occurs, but the prospective parent dies before adoption finalization.

**Employer Assistance:** Adoption benefits offered by an employer to an employee. These may include cash assistance to cover adoption expenses, reimbursement of approved adoption expenses, and paid or unpaid family leave.

**FBI Criminal Clearances:** Part of a home study report conducted by the FBI and involving the fingerprinting of every adult in a prospective adoptive home. The cost is nominal. Not all states require such clearance, but it may be required by the birth mother's state prior to an adoption.

**Family Preservation:** A program of supportive social services with the goal of keeping birth families together by providing services to children and parents. The program is based on the premise that birth families are the preferred means of providing family life for children.

**Fathers' Adoption Registry:** A listing created for putative fathers who wish to receive notice from the court if plans are made to place their children for adoption. A man may register before the child is born, but must register within thirty days of the child's birth to ensure that his rights are protected.

**Finalization:** The last legal step in the adoption process. Finalization involves a court hearing during which the judge orders the adoption decree, which states that the adoptive parents are the child's permanent, legal parents. The time this court hearing takes place differs by law from state to state.

**Facilitator:** See *Adoption Facilitator*.

**Foster Adoption/Fost-Adopt/Fos-Adopt:** A form of adoption in which a child who is unlikely to be reunited with his or her birth family is placed in a foster home and eventually adopted by the foster parents. This term also refers to a child placement in which the birth parents' rights have not yet been severed by the court, or the birth parents are appealing the court's decision, and the foster parents have agreed to adopt the child if and when parental rights are terminated. The main reason for making such a placement — also called legal risk adoption — is to keep the child from being moved from place to place.

**Foster Care:** A temporary arrangement, either informal or arranged through a social services agency or court, in which persons other than the birth parents care for a child for a period of time.

**Foster Care Plan:** A written plan detailing why a child is in foster care and how long the child will need to remain there. The plan usually includes timelines and requirements for either birth family reunification or eventual adoption.

**Foster Children:** Children who have been placed in the state or county's legal custody because their parents or caregivers are deemed abusive, neglectful, or otherwise unable to care for them.

**Foster Parents:** Individuals or couples, licensed by the state or county, who have temporary care of a child but no legal rights to determine certain aspects of that child's life. Foster parents occasionally become adoptive parents. The goal of foster care is to return a child to the family of origin unless the courts decide it is not in the child's best interest to do so.

**Grief:** Deep mental anguish, often experienced as the result of a loss; sorrow; a feeling of emotional deprivation. All members of the adoption triad may experience grief.

**Group Home:** A residence in which several unrelated children live for varying time periods. Group homes may have one set of house parents or a rotating staff.

**Guardian:** A person who is legally responsible for the care and management of a minor child. The courts or birth parents may continue to hold some jurisdiction over the child. Guardians do not have the same reciprocal rights of inheritance as birth and adoptive parents. Guardianship is subject to ongoing supervision by the court and ends when the child reaches legal age or by order of the court.

**Guardian Ad Litem:** Citizens or attorneys who volunteer to become part of a court program to represent the best interests of an abused or neglected child who is the subject of judicial proceedings. A guardian ad litem serves as the child's representative before the court, social service agencies, and the community. He or she also protects the child during the family crisis and court proceedings, and follows the child's progress after the court disposes of the case. The legal protective status of a guardian ad litem exists only within the confines of the particular court case in which the appointment was made.

**Hague Convention:** The Hague Convention on Intercountry Adoption is a multilateral treaty designed to apply to all international adoptions between countries that ratify it. It is the result of a five-year process involving participants from 66 prospective member countries. Under the terms of the treaty, an adoption may take place only if:

- The country of origin establishes that the child is adoptable

- It is deemed that an intercountry adoption is in the child's best interests

- After counseling, the necessary consent to the adoption is given freely

- The receiving country determines that the prospective adoptive parents are eligible and suited to adopt

- The child they wish to adopt is authorized to enter and reside permanently in that country

Every country must establish a national government-level central authority to carry out certain non-delegable functions that include cooperating with other central authorities, overseeing the implementation of the Convention in its country, and providing information on the laws of its country.

**Home Study:** See *Adoption Home Study Report.*

**I-600 and I-600A Visa Petition:** An official request to the U.S. Immigration and Naturalization Service (INS) to classify an orphan as an immediate relative, providing expedited processing and issuance of a visa to allow the child to enter the United States after having been adopted abroad or in order to be adopted in the United States.

**I-600A--Application for Advance Processing of Orphan Petition:** A form filed with the U.S. Immigration and Naturalization Service (INS) by prospective adoptive parents in order to receive approval to bring a child from another country into the United States for the purposes of adoption. Parents must submit the I-600A with photocopies of their birth certificates, marriage certificate (if applicable), and divorce decree (if applicable), as well as two fingerprint cards per person (completed by an authorized fingerprinting agency) and the appropriate fee. An adoption home study report must be received by INS before approval will be given.

**Identified Adoption:** A situation in which a couple or family who wishes to adopt locates a birth mother or birth parents who are making an adoption plan for their child. With the help of friends, family, a physician, an attorney, or an adoption professional such as a facilitator, adoptive parents and birth parents find each other and proceed to an agency or an attorney to complete the adoption process.

**Identifying Information:** Data on birth parents or members of their families, adoptive parents, or adoptees that leads to the disclosure of their identities.

**Income Statement:** A determination of financial stability. The home study poses questions that will help determine if prospective adoptive parents can reasonably afford to meet the needs of a child. Income verification may take the form of paycheck stubs, a W-4 form, or an income tax form (1040 or 1040 EZ). Details will be gathered regarding savings, insurance policies, and other investments and debts, including monthly mortgage or rent payment, car loans, and credit card payments.

**Independent Adoption:** An adoption facilitated by someone other than a caseworker associated with an agency. Independent adoption is handled by attorneys, adoption facilitators, and other intermediaries, and is not allowed in all states.

**Indian Child Welfare Act:** A federal law regarding the placement of Native American children. The act establishes the tribe's sovereignty as a separate nation over the welfare of children who are tribal members or who are eligible for tribal membership.

**Infertility:** The inability to bear or carry a child to term. Secondary infertility refers to a situation wherein one child is born, but a secondary pregnancy does not occur.

**INS:** U.S. Immigration and Naturalization Service, a federal agency under the Justice Department that oversees all visas issued to allow entry into the United States. This agency is responsible for reviewing documents and issuing approval for a child adopted from a country outside the U.S. to immigrate to the United States.

**I-171H--Notice of Favorable Determination Concerning Application for Advance Processing of Orphan Petition:** A document received from the INS after successful filing of form I-600A Application for Advance Processing of Orphan Petition. This is a lengthy process that can take up to several months to complete. (An FBI fingerprint check alone can take up to three months or longer.) However, this extended timeframe is not always the case and varies considerably from state to state.

**IR-3 and IR-4 Visas:** An IR-3 visa is for orphans who are adopted in their birth country and then immigrate to the United States. An IR-4 visa is for orphans whose adoptions are finalized in U.S. state courts after immigration to the U.S. The regulations of the birth country determine which procedure is used. U.S. State Department data on international adoptions is based on the number of visas issued to children adopted from other countries by U.S. citizens, although technically the visa data tracks the immigration of the children to the U.S., not their adoptions.

**Institutionalization:** The placement of children in hospitals, institutions, or orphanages. Some experts suggest that such placement during critical developmental stages and for lengthy periods may be associated with developmental delays due to environmental deprivation, poor staff-child ratios, and/or lack of early stimulation.

**Intercountry or International Adoption:** The adoption of a child who is a citizen of one country by parents who are citizens of a different country. Legal work through immigration services must be done to authorize an international adoption, and approval must be obtained from both domestic and foreign governments. Travel by the adoptive parents may or may not be required. International adoption should be conducted by a reputable agency.

**Interstate Compact on the Placement of Children (ICPC):** An agreement that regulates the placement of children across state lines. All fifty states, plus the District of Columbia and the U.S. Virgin Islands, have independently adopted the ICPC as statutory law in their respective jurisdictions. The ICPC must give its approval to any child moving from one state to another for the purpose of adoption, foster care, or residential care. The ICPC 100A form must be approved by both the child's state of origin (sending state) and the state where the child will live (receiving state) before the child can legally cross state lines. In an interstate adoption, the agency or attorney from the state where the child resides is most often responsible for processing the interstate paperwork.

**Interstate Compact on Adoption and Medical Assistance (ICAMA):** An agreement between member states that governs the interstate delivery of, and payment for, medical services and adoption assistance payments/subsidies for adopted children with special needs. The agreements are established by the laws of the states that are members of the compact.

**Interethnic Placement:** Refers to Section 1808 of P.L. 104-188, Removal of Barriers to Interethnic Adoption, which affirms the prohibition contained in the Multi-Ethnic Placement Act of 1994 against delaying or denying the placement of a child for adoption or foster care on the basis of race, color, or national origin of the foster or adoptive parents or the child involved.

**Involuntary Termination of Parental Rights:** A legal procedure wherein the legal rights of the birth parents are terminated by the court without their signed consent. Decisions for such action are based on the needs of the child. Examples for such decisions include abandonment, repeated or severe abuse, and neglect.

**Kinship Care:** Full-time care and nurturing of a child provided by a member of the child's extended biological family.

**Kinship Adoption:** A form of adoption wherein the adoptive parents are biologically related to the adopted child—such as grandparents, aunts and uncles, or other relatives. In kinship adoption, the relatives legally adopt the child.

**Learning Disabled:** A term used to describe a child who has difficulty with reading, math, and/or writing skills, and who performs below the age-appropriate level in school or other activities. Children with learning disabilities may be of average or above average intelligence, but experience difficulty with learning, differentiating, processing, storing, and/or making use of information. Some children with learning disabilities find it difficult to learn in a conventional classroom environment. Learning disabilities are as common in the general population as they are among children who are adopted. Parents who educate themselves about learning disabilities through study and interaction with other parents will be able to help their adopted children by working with them and finding appropriate special education.

**Legal Custody/ Legal Guardian:** Responsibility for a person according to law—such as a guardian's authority—conferred by the court over a person or property or both. When a minor child is involved, it includes care and responsibility for the child and his or her property.

**Legalized Abandonment:** A law, applicable in some states, that legalizes the anonymous abandonment of infants at predetermined drop centers.

**Legal Risk Adoption:** An adoption wherein the child to be adopted is placed with the prospective adoptive parents prior to the termination of the birth parents' rights. In such instances, the birth parents can revoke their consent to the adoption and have the child returned to them. The legal risk period is determined by each state. Legal risk adoptions are rare in special-needs adoption.

**Legal Risk Placement:** Placement of a child in a prospective adoptive family when a child is not yet legally free for adoption. In such cases, it is expected that the family will eventually adopt the child, even though the birth parents' rights have not been fully terminated or the parents are contesting the legal action.

**Legally Free:** A child who is available for adoption because the birth parents' rights have been legally terminated.

**Life Book:** A record of text and pictures that chronicles the life of a child. This book helps the child understand and appreciate his or her unique background and history. It may include birth parents, other relatives, foster parents and their families, homes where they child has lived, and childhood experiences and events.

**Long-Term Foster Care:** The intentional and planned placement of a child in foster care for an extended period of time. After adoption has been explored and rejected, after placement with relatives has been considered and found unfeasible, long-term foster care may be seen as a viable option. This plan is increasingly viewed by some state's child welfare systems as a poor placement alternative.

**Loss:** A state of grief experienced when deprived of someone or something of value. Almost all of those involved in adoption experience a sense of loss at some time in their lives.

**Matching:** The act of locating and connecting a birth mother and a family interested in completing an adoption plan. This term is not to be confused with "placement."

**Maternity Home:** A residence maintained by a non-profit or private organization for the purpose of providing a residence for unmarried pregnant women.

**Multi-Ethnic Placement Act:** A federal law enacted in 1994 and implemented through state policy. This act prohibits the delay or denial of any adoption or placement in foster care due to the race, color, or national origin of the child or the foster or adoptive parents, and requires states to provide for diligent recruitment of potential foster and adoptive families who reflect the ethnic and racial diversity of children for whom homes are needed. The 1996 amendment—the Removal of Barriers to Interethnic Adoption Act—affirms the prohibition.

**Non-Identifying Information:** Facts about birth or adoptive parents that would not lead to their discovery by another person. Such non-identifying information is usually limited to age, physical description, talents and hobbies, and basic medical data. State laws vary regarding the release and definition of non-identifying information. Cost, as well as the amount of information received, depends on the agency or court that releases the information.

**Non-Recurring Adoption Costs:** One-time adoption expenses, which, through the provisions of the Adoption Assistance and Child Welfare Act of 1980, may be at least partially reimbursed by the state to families adopting children with special needs. Allowable expenses for this reimbursement benefit can include the cost of a home study, adoption fees, court costs, attorney fees, physical and psychological examinations, travel to visit with the child prior to the placement, and other expenses related to the legal adoption of a child with special needs.

**North American Council on Adoptable Children:** Founded in 1974 by adoptive parents, the North American Council on Adoptable Children is committed to meeting the needs of waiting children and the families who adopt them. Since its inception, NACAC's mission has remained essentially unchanged, advocating the right of every child to a permanent, continuous, nurturing, and culturally sensitive family.

**National Council for Adoption:** An organization operating at local, state, national, and international levels to help build happy families.

**Open Adoption:** An adoption that allows the birth mother or birth parents to have a choice about the family adopting their child. In open adoption, a wide range of options are available, including, but not limited to: meetings between families before or after the birth of the child, the presence of the adoptive parents at the birth of the child, the continuation of relationship between families through various combinations of letters, photos, videos, gifts, and personal visits. See *Cooperative Adoption*.

**Open Records:** Accessibility to adoption records, including identifying information, by all members of the adoption triad.

**Orphan:** A child under the age of 18 whose parents have died, have relinquished their parental rights, or have had their rights terminated by the courts.

**Orphanage:** An institution that houses children who are orphaned, abandoned, or whose parents are unable to care for them. Orphanages are used frequently abroad but rarely in the United States, where group homes are the preferred alternative.

**Orphan (international adoption definition for immigration purposes):** A child under the age of sixteen whose parents have died or are not in touch with the child; a child who has been separated from the parents through abandonment or whose sole surviving parent is impoverished by local standards and incapable of providing that child with proper care, and who has, in writing, irrevocably released the child for emigration and adoption.

**Parties to an Adoption:** A child legally free to be adopted, and a person or persons eligible to adopt.

**Passive Reunion Registry:** A centralized place where birth parents and adult adoptees can register their identifying information and request to be notified if other parties in their adoption also register. In cases where data is incorrect, a match cannot be made. Some states have state-run registries, and there are also privately sponsored registries such as the Soundex Registry.

**Paternity Testing:** Genetic testing that can determine the identity of a child's biological father.

**Permanency Planning:** The process of working to help children live in permanent families. The goal is to provide the child with loving and nurturing parents or caretakers and the opportunity to establish lifelong family relationships.

**Photo Listing Book:** Resources, available both online and in book form, that contain photos and descriptions of waiting children available for adoption.

**Placement Date:** The date a child begins to live with adopting parents.

**Post-Adoption Services:** Case management services, referrals for counseling, or other supportive services available to families after finalization of an adoption.

**Post-Placement Supervision:** Counseling and supervision provided by a licensed social worker to the adopted parents and child subsequent to the child's adoptive placement and before the adoption is legally finalized in court. Reports made during this time are presented to the court of jurisdiction.

**Post-Reunion Issues:** The feelings and thoughts that occur when members of the adoption triad experience both the joy and grief that occur after reconnecting through reunion.

**Pre-Certification:** Court approval of a prospective adoptive parent granted upon review of the home study, references, child abuse clearance, fingerprints, medical status, employment verification, and other documents. Upon such approval, the court issues a certificate—which which remains with the court—stating that the person(s) can adopt a child. The necessary paperwork is submitted by an attorney and is typically required for an agency adoption.

**Private Adoption:** An adoption arranged without the involvement of an agency, or an adoption facilitated by people or agencies that are privately funded. An intermediary, such as an adoption facilitator or attorney, is involved. A private adoption can be an open adoption, although that is not always the case. Private adoptions should not be confused with private agency adoptions. See *Independent Adoption*.

**Private Agency Adoption:** Placements made by licensed organizations that screen prospective adoptive parents and supervise the placement of children in adoptive homes until the adoption is finalized. Private agencies serve the needs of both birth families and adoptive families and may be nonprofit or for-profit agencies.

**Psychological Parent:** A person not biologically related to a child whom the child considers a parent; sometimes referred to as a "de facto" parent.

**Public Agency Adoption:** An adoption facilitated by the Department of Human Services, also known as the Office of Children and Youth Services. This agency places children who come into its care either voluntarily or involuntarily. It is responsible for most adoptions of older children and for handling cases where children have been abused, neglected, or abandoned by their birth parents.

**Putative Father:** The legal term for the alleged or supposed father of a child. It refers to a man who may be a child's biological father, but who is not married to the child's mother on or before the date the child was or is to be born, and/or has not established paternity of the child in a court proceeding.

**Putative Father Registries:** A registry system that ensures the protection of a birth father's rights. Some states require that birth fathers register, while others presume that a birth father does not wish to pursue paternity rights if he does not initiate legal action. States generally require a putative father to register or acknowledge paternity within a certain time frame in order to receive notice of adoption proceedings. Approximately twenty-one states have statutes authorizing the establishment of putative father registries. Several states, however, only mandate by law that a putative father file a notice of his paternity claim within a certain period of time. Failure to register or file may preclude the right to notice of adoption proceedings.

**Relinquishment:** Voluntary termination of parental rights, sometimes referred to as surrender or making an adoption plan for one's child. This is a process by which birth parents willingly terminate their parental rights in order to free their child for adoption. It is a legally binding, permanent procedure involving the signing of documents and court action.

**Residential Care Facility:** A 24-hour care facility with staff that provides psychological services to help troubled children.

**Residential Treatment:** Treatment at a facility to assist those who are unable to function satisfactorily in their own homes. For children and adolescents, residential treatment tends to be the option of choice when a child is considered to be in danger of hurting himself or others.

**Respite Care:** Temporary or short-term child care that occurs outside the child's home and is provided by an adult or adults other than the child's birth, foster, or adoptive parents.

**Reunion:** A post-adoption meeting between an adoptee and a member or members of his or her birth family.

**Reunion Registry:** See *Passive Reunion Registry* and *Voluntary Adoption Registry*.

**Reunification:** The attempt to return foster children to the custody of their parent(s) after placement outside the home.

**Reunification Services:** A process through which social service agency workers help birth families find solutions to problems so the family can live together.

**Revocation of Consent:** A legal process whereby a birth parent revokes the consent he or she signed to an adoption plan and requests that the child be returned to his or her custody. In states that allow revocation of consent, there is a limited period of time for the parent to choose this option. State laws vary and are constantly changing.

**Search/Adoption Search:** An attempt to make contact between the birth parent and the biological child. This attempt is usually made by the birth parent, adopted person, or adoptive parent.

**Search and Consent Procedures:** Procedures available for the consensual disclosure of identifying information. A "confidential intermediary service" is available to help adoptees over the age of twenty-one and biological relatives locate each other and ascertain whether they are willing to release their names or have personal contact with each other.

**Semi-Open Adoption:** An adoption in which the birth and adoptive parents establish the extent of some type of limited, ongoing contact between the birth parents and the child. This can take many forms and is commonly facilitated through letters and photos.

**Special-Needs Adoption:** The adoption of a child with particular needs or challenges. Adoptions of this type generally involve more extensive training on the part of the parents, and fees are lower or nonexistent. Special-needs children include older children, sibling groups, children facing physical, emotional, or intellectual challenges, and children of mixed race or minorities. Federal and state subsidies are sometimes available to parents who adopt special-needs children.

**SSI Benefits:** A Social Security Administration program that provides financial support to persons—including children—with specific, defined handicapping conditions. After an adoption is finalized, these benefits are tied to the adoptive parent's income.

**Stepparent Adoption:** The adoption of a child by the spouse of the birth parent.

**Subsidy:** See *Adoption Assistance Payment.*

**Substitute Care:** Any kind of care, sanctioned by the court of jurisdiction in which a child lives, with someone other than the birth parent.

**Surrender:** See *Relinquishment.*

**Surrender Papers:** Legal documents attesting to the voluntary relinquishment of parental rights to a child.

**Surrogate Mother:** A woman who carries and bears a child for another woman or a couple by pre-arrangement and legal contract.

**System:** Refers to the public child welfare system, which is a network of governmental agencies and services that provides for children in its jurisdiction.

**Termination of Parental Rights:** A process involving a court hearing whereby a judge enters a decree that permanently ends all legal parental rights of a birth parent. Termination of parental rights can be voluntary or involuntary and must occur before a child is considered to be legally free for adoption.

**Therapeutic (or Treatment) Foster Home:** A foster home in which the caregivers have received training to care for a diversity of children and adolescents, usually those with significant emotional or behavioral problems. Parents in therapeutic foster homes are more closely supervised and receive more assistance than parents in regular foster homes.

**Traditional Adoption:** A domestic infant adoption in which confidentiality is preserved. This is also known as closed adoption.

**Traditional Agency Adoption:** An adoption facilitated by an agency that locates a birth mother, counsels her, and provides assistance for an adoption to take place. The birth mother may or may not pick the prospective adoptive parents from biographical resumes, and the adoptive parents may or may not have contact with the birth parents.

**U.S. Adoption Laws:** Laws with which persons contemplating adoption must comply. In general, adoption issues are subject to state laws and regulations. State adoption laws are comprised of laws from two sources: state statutes and state case law.

**Voluntary Adoption Registry:** A reunion registry system that assists adoptees, birth parents, and biological siblings to locate each other by maintaining a voluntary list of adoptees and birth relatives.

**Voluntary Placement Agreement (VPA):** An agreement made through the courts or a social service agency with the parents of a child who must remain in foster care while the family meets certain requirements specifically outlined in the agreement. If the agreement and plan are not successful, the child may be removed permanently and placed for adoption.

**Voluntary Termination of Parental Rights:** The voluntary relinquishment of parental rights by birth parents who willingly create an adoption plan and legally free a child for adoption.

**Waiting Children:** Children in need of permanent, loving adoptive homes. They are usually older, in the public child welfare system, and cannot return to their birth families. Waiting children are also considered special-needs children.

**Waiting Period:** The time, prior to placement, during which a family is approved for adoption by an agency.

**Waiver of Confidentiality:** A document filed by a person allowing for disclosure of records or identifying information to another person.

# HELPFUL RESOURCES

## Online Adoption Professionals

Lifetime Adoption Center      www.LifetimeAdoption.com

Christian Adoption Online      www.ChristianAdoptionOnline.com

Catholic Adoption      www.CatholicAdoptionOnline.com

Open Adoption      www.OpenAdoption.com

African American Adoptions Online      www.AAAdoptions.com

Bi-Racial Adoptions      www.Biracial-Adoptions.com

State by State Adoptions      www.StateByStateAdoptions.com

## Adoption Help & Education

Adoption Prayer Bracelet      www.MyAdoptionPrayer.com

Lifetime Adoption Foundation      www.LifetimeFoundation.org

Adoption Financing      www.AdoptionFinancingInformation.com

Adoption Teleconference      www.AdoptionTeleconference.com

Let's Talk Adoption      www.LetsTalkAdoption.com

Adoption For Life Newsletter      www.AdoptionForLife.com

Adoption Home Study Report      www.AdoptionHomeStudyReport.com

International Adoption      www.AskAboutInternationalAdoption.com

## Books

So I Was Thinking About Adoption      www.IWasThinkingAboutAdoption.com

Adoption: Your Step by Step Guide      www.AdoptionStepByStep.com

Adoption Love Stories      www.AdoptionLoveStories.com

## Resources

Better Business Bureau Online      www.BBBOnline.org

U.S. Government International
Adoption Information      www.adoption.gov.info

IRS Adoption Tax Credit      www.irs.gov/taxtopics/tc607

# ABOUT THE AUTHORS

## MARDIE CALDWELL

**Mardie Caldwell**, C.O.A.P., is a nationally-recognized authority on adoption. A Certified Open Adoption Practitioner, Caldwell founded Lifetime Adoption Center in 1986. She has assisted in over 3,000 successful adoptions nationwide.

Photo courtesy of Borel Photography

Caldwell is dedicated to educating and helping birth parents and adoptive parents through teaching, motivational speaking, writing, and being the talk show host of *Let's Talk Adoption*. Author of a number of award winning books, Caldwell has made more than 200 appearances on television, including NBC's The Today Show, The 700 Club, The Larry King Show, CNN, Fox, ABC, CBS, PBS, BBC, CBN, and The Dr. Laura Show. She has been featured on hundreds of national radio shows and is widely sought for print articles.

As a Christian and adoptive mom, Caldwell believes the path that lead her to adopt was God preparing her for the work she does today in adoption.

## HEATHER FEATHERSTON

**Heather Featherston** has a passion for working with women and families facing issues surrounding pregnancy, adoption, and parenting. She is currently the Director of Adoption Services at Lifetime Adoption Center, overseeing the coordination of services for thousands of clients nationwide.

Photo courtesy of Elizabeth Murray

Featherston has spoken to professional groups, conducted trainings for birth parent advocates, and has made television and radio appearances discussing various aspects of adoption. She has supported, one-on-one, couples working through adoption decisions and discerning the Lord's will.

As an adoption professional, Featherston is in awe of seeing God's hand at work each day, guiding children and families together through adoption.

# QUICK ORDER FORM

**Order online:** CalledToAdoption.com
**Email orders:** info@CarriageHousePublishing.com
**Fax orders:** 1-877-423-6783
**Telephone orders:** 1-877-423-6785

**Postal orders:** American Carriage House Publishing
P.O. Box 1130, Nevada City, CA 95959

Name_____

Address_____

City_____ State_____ Zip_____

Telephone_____

Email Address_____

Cost per book: US $12.95

Sales tax: Please add 8.375% for products shipped to California addresses.

Shipping: US $4.95 for first book, $1.00 for each additional copy

International: US $9.95 for first book, $4.00 for each additional copy (may vary depending on destination)

Payment:   ☐ Check   ☐ Credit Card

Card Number_____

Name on card_____

Exp. Date_____ Security Code_____

**Please contact the publisher at 1-877-423-6785 for volume discounts**

# QUICK ORDER FORM

**Order online**: CalledToAdoption.com
**Email orders**: info@CarriageHousePublishing.com
**Fax orders**: 1-877-423-6783
**Telephone orders**: 1-877-423-6785

**Postal orders**: American Carriage House Publishing
P.O. Box 1130, Nevada City, CA 95959

Name_____

Address_____

City_____ State_____ Zip_____

Telephone_____

Email Address_____

Cost per book: US $12.95

Sales tax: Please add 8.375% for products shipped to California addresses.

Shipping: US $4.95 for first book, $1.00 for each additional copy

International: US $9.95 for first book, $4.00 for each additional copy (may vary depending on destination)

Payment:    ☐ Check    ☐ Credit Card

Card Number_____

Name on card_____

Exp. Date_____ Security Code_____

**Please contact the publisher at 1-877-423-6785 for volume discounts**

HOW HAS
# CALLED TO ADOPTION
## INSPIRED YOU?

• • •

Have you discovered scripture
that has encouraged or helped
as you take steps to build your family?

Do you have scripture that would help
others waiting for a child?

• • •

*Let us know!*

Go online and share what has helped and
inspired you in God's plan for your family.

**www.CalledToAdoption.com/HisWord**

*"Your word is a lamp to my feet
and a light for my path."*
Psalm 119:105